Michael Carotta

SOMETIMES WE
DANCE
SOMETIMES WE
WRESTLE

Embracing the
Spiritual Growth
of Adolescents

Harcourt
Religion Publishers

Harcourt
Religion Publishers

Our Mission

The primary mission of Harcourt Religion Publishers is to provide
the Catholic and Christian educational markets with the highest
quality catechetical print and media resources. The content of these
resources reflects the best insights of current theology, methodology,
and pedagogical research. The resources are practical and easy
to use, designed to meet expressed market needs, and written to
reflect the teachings of the Catholic Church.

Printed in the United States of America

ISBN 0-15-901046-2

10 9 8 7 6 5 4 3

This book is dedicated to every veteran teacher, counselor, coach, administrator, youth minister, and volunteer who has *intentionally* sustained a life committed to the well-being of young people in our classrooms, clinics, community centers, and churches,

and

to each new person who has made a decision to do so.

Acknowledgements

A debt of gratitude is owed to Matthew J. Thibeau for seeing the value of publishing this work.

I also want to thank Bishop Thomas Kelly and his staff at the Louisville Office of Lifelong Formation for supporting my doctoral studies and Spalding University's Dr. Angela Shaughnessy and Dr. John Shaughnessy for their guidance on this project.

Most of the inspiration behind this work comes from soulful conversations with over one hundred dedicated and passionate private and public school educators who participated in the five different Teaching for Spiritual Growth Summer Institutes. I particularly want to thank Dr. Margaret Guider of the Weston Jesuit School of Theology for her mentoring, Dr. Francis Butler and the members of FADICA for funding the Institutes, and Dr. Robert Coles of Harvard, who continuously showed me the power of stories firsthand.

I wish I knew how to acknowledge countless colleagues I have learned from over the years at conferences via late-night discussions that went into early morning.

But the greatest joy has come from sharing the development of this work with my wife Catherine, whose insight, honesty, love, laughter, and listening ear is a gift to all who know her.

Contents

Introduction

This book outlines four different ways in which interested adults can intentionally participate in the spiritual growth of adolescents. It describes three different dimensions of adolescent spirituality, takes a critical look at developmental theories of the past, exposes the myth of self-esteem, and reminds us that *we were never their age.* More than a collection of anecdotes, the book blends supporting research from various disciplines with stories and real-life examples gleaned from twenty-five years of experience. It is hoped that counselors, teachers, ministers, at-risk specialists, coaches, parents, aunts and uncles, administrators, and any other faith-filled adults will recognize, and have confidence in, the spiritual growth activity that best suits her or his natural interests and personality.

Without needing specialized training, degrees, titles, personality traits, or expertise, you will be able to recognize the dominant dimension of spirituality in the young persons for whom you care and will learn how to actively help them move forward on their spiritual journey.

Chapter 1

Fishing the River

Several years ago, I was asked by the University of Notre Dame to come and review a new program they had developed in which graduates could volunteer as teachers in the rural areas of the South and also earn a master's degree in education. After my meeting, I decided to check out the great fishing for lake trout that takes place every fall in the nearby St. Joe River.

I awoke at 5:30 A.M. in order to get to the river by 6:30. I spent my first hour there asking questions in the local tackle shop. How long of a rod? What kind of reel? What weight of line? What kind of lure? The answer to every question invariably included a warning: Fishing the river was incredibly difficult, and the trout were both strong and smart. Only the seasoned and well-schooled angler had success fishing this powerful river for such hard-to-catch fish.

I learned that the rod had to be a certain length, with just the right combination of flexibility and backbone. Fiberglass spinning rods would not do. Instead, graphite rods were recommended. They were lighter, stronger, and more sensitive—allowing one to feel the slightest tug.

Nor would conventional spinning reels hold up. I was told that the reel should have at least three or four stainless-steel ball bearings in order to deliver the smoothness and strength necessary to withstand the fight of these cagey fish once hooked in the river's mighty currents.

The fishing line had to be both strong and supple. No ordinary line would do. The line must be strong enough not to break when the fisher set the hook, abrasion-resistant enough to handle the wear of the river's rocks and sand, and yet limp enough to fly through the air when casting the lure. Finally, it had to be extremely supple, so as not to impede the natural action of the lure when it was being reeled in.

The lure itself, of course, was the most important of all. To catch the fish in this rugged river, a lure had to be a certain shape, color, and material. It had to swim with just the right motion, at just the right depth, and be reeled in at just the right speed. Even the size of the hook on the lure was important. If the hook was too small, the fish would free itself. If it was too big, the fish would notice it and not take the lure.

All of these details and specifics made sense. This approach to fishing was complicated to the point of being almost scientific. The anglers were right: Fishing the river was incredibly hard, and its trout were both strong and smart. Only the seasoned and well-schooled angler would have success fishing this powerful river for such hard-to-catch fish.

After spending an hour gathering all this information, I left the tackle shop empty-handed and hurried to the banks of the river in hopes of seeing anglers. It was dawn, and the fishing, I thought, should be good. I noticed three men fishing on a sand bar in the middle of the river, about 75 yards from shore. With my Styrofoam coffee cup in hand, I quickly skipped along the rocks to the sandbar. The three anglers looked as if they hadn't shaved in days. They seemed solemn and spoke very little. Their eyes intently followed their lures as they cast them into the strong and flowing river and retrieved them. I explained that I was a surf angler and did not know how to fish this river. I began asking questions, and, to my astonishment, these seasoned anglers responded. My ego soared. I convinced myself that they answered my questions because they knew that I knew fishing.

For three days the men had been fishing, with the correct rods, reels, line, and lures. At night they slept in the back of their truck. Three days ago one of them had caught a fish. Yesterday each of the two others had caught one. And just about an hour ago another fish had gotten away. How I wanted to see one of those beautiful fish! It was true: Fishing the river was incredibly hard, and the trout were both strong and smart. Only the seasoned and well-schooled angler had success fishing this powerful river for such hard to-catch-fish.

After fifteen minutes, I thanked these anglers, wished them luck, and walked back across the rocks. Just before reaching shore, I happened to glance down the riverbank to my right. Two people—one, a child in a yellow slicker—were fishing about a football field away. I sensed something happening there; I took a long look before getting into my car and noticed one of them reeling in something splashing across the water. They had caught a fish! I literally ran down the bank in my excitement.

When I got there, I asked the ten-year-old girl in the yellow slicker, who was beaming and giggling, if she had caught the fish. She smiled and said that her grandfather had caught it and that he was the best angler. Both were Vietnamese. I watched her grandfather pull in a large, shiny, beautiful lake trout with a toy-like fishing rod. He had the reel upside down and was actually using it backwards. I could feel the joy these two anglers shared as they smiled and giggled. I, too, smiled and congratulated them on their catch. Such a beautiful fish. As the child's grandfather unhooked the fish, he pulled a rope out of the water. One end of the rope was tied to a small tree on the riverbank, and the other was submerged in the water. The rope held two more beautiful fish, which Grandfather and his granddaughter had caught earlier.

I asked how long the two had been fishing. With a big grin and in broken English, the man replied that he and his granddaughter had been fishing for about an hour and a half. The two explained that when they caught a fish, they squeezed out its eggs out and wrapped them in cheesecloth to form little balls. Then they simply tied a ball of eggs onto their line with a hook and sinker, cast it into the river, let it sink to the bottom, and waited for the fish to come. At home, they kept the eggs in a jar in the refrigerator until they were ready to go fishing again.

Grandfather showed me his simple plastic tackle box. He had several wads of cheesecloth neatly wrapped in a rubber band and labeled with writing scrawled on pieces of brown paper. Everything was neatly organized and simple.

I took it all in and praised the grandfather and his granddaughter for their fishing skills. As I turned to leave, I was struck by the sight of the three anglers fishing on the sandbar with all their gear, hoping to outsmart a fish or two in the next few days. The irony and contrast between the two sets of anglers left me numb.

On the way home, I realized that I, too, had caught a great fish, although my catch was not one that swims, but instead was one that teaches a lesson and offers a glimpse of truth.

This story illustrates two different methods of fishing. One approach tries to outsmart the fish, while the other attempts to be with the fish. One method uses artificial means of imitation—factory-made lure—while the other uses what the river gives—the eggs of fishes caught. One way of fishing sees the river as an obstacle, while the other views it as an opportunity to be mined.

One group of anglers take a high-tech approach, while the grandfather and his granddaughter take a low-tech one. For the first group, fishing is solemn and almost stoic. It is an experience of study and sport. For the others, it is joyful and almost playful—an experience of family. There are other contrasts and comparisons as well.

If the river symbolized adolescent spiritual growth, which anglers best represent the way you would "fish the river"?

What makes you come to that conclusion?

This book describes an approach to embracing adolescent spiritual growth that is more like the man and child using what the river gives them than the more professional approach taken by the other anglers.

Yet both ways of "fishing the river" require you and I to have a certain degree of intentionality.

This book also offers you a way of "fishing the river" of adolescent spiritual growth that transcends professional training, job titles, and religious affiliation, is easily understood, and allows caring adults to utilize their individual interests and styles. It can be described as a model of teaching because it involves an intentional and sustained effort to help adolescents grow in their spirituality.

The models of facilitating adolescent spirituality that have evolved from 1968 through 1998 have consisted of retreats, formal religious instruction, informal youth groups, youth-friendly worship services, creative prayer experiences, outreach initiatives, evangelization, relational ministry, peer ministry, outdoor challenge programs, church-sponsored athletics, and service-learning experiences. Some of these models continue to be employed effectively among adolescents.

However the approaches offered in the following pages are not restricted to formal methods of teaching and instruction but encompass a more informal kind of teaching that has been modeled for generations by guides, sponsors, mentors, coaches, elders, and parents. At the same time, this work will attempt to reflect the real and rich nature of relationships and interactions between adolescents and adults.

Crisis of the Spirit

Today's churches and parents care about the spiritual growth of young people; formal religious instruction is an expectation within the American experience of growing up. What's more, our society seems to be increasingly interested in the moral dimension of adolescent culture. This country has given birth to national programs promoting adolescent chastity, sobriety, prayer, and community service. Recent movies and TV shows dealing with spiritual topics ranging from angels to afterlife are popular and profitable. Books focusing on taking care of the adult soul and nurturing our spirituality show up on the *New York Times* best-sellers list. Poll after poll shows that Americans pray and believe. We have a spiritual hunger.[1]

However many spiritual ironies and contradictions that have long troubled humanity have taken on a contemporary appearance. Some of us "take care of the soul" *and* cheat on taxes. Parents give to charity *and* curse the referee. Teenagers pray *and* have sex. Young gang members wear religious symbols around their necks *and* engage in violent acts. Other young people avoid attending church *and* build homes for the needy.

Adolescents should not be viewed as potential problems but as resilient and fragile gifts of passion and promise in need of principles.

Because they are entrusted to adults to learn from and to be led, it is possible for all to participate intentionally in the spiritual growth of adolescents. This book will offer concrete suggestions for walking with young people on their spiritual journey.

The developmental theories of Piaget, Kohlberg, Erikson, and Fowler, which once were held up as models for understanding the human journey of moral and religious growth, are now considered to be limited and incomplete. These theories of development are debated, critiqued, and enhanced. Robert Kegan, for example, identifies several "neglects" within Piaget's model. Kegan points out that such developmental models focus on cognition to the neglect of emotion. The models focus on the individual and neglect the social, the stages of development and neglect the processes of development, and how a person changes to the neglect of how a person persists.[2] Others have come to agree.[3]

It is time to address spiritual growth in terms of *dimensions* rather than developmental stages.

As young people navigate an unprecedented journey through adolescence in the new millennium, adults interested in participating in the spiritual growth of young people are faced with a variety of approaches, strategies, goals, and programs, most of which appear to require specialized training, education, or professional roles. Consequently, caring adults, already stressed by their own race through contemporary life, may find it too complex, unclear, or time-consuming to walk intentionally with adolescents on their spiritual path. Adults who were once willing and able to donate the considerable amount of time required to support the youth-serving models of the 1980s and '90s now are "in over their [our] heads" as they deal with the mental demands of modern life.[4]

In addition, youth culture today is not what it was a decade ago. Facilitating adolescent spiritual growth has become something adults view as very complex and nuanced, much the way "fishing the river" can be viewed as a challenge requiring great study, skills, equipment, and endurance. Interested adults have become reluctant to fish the river of adolescent spiritual growth, preferring to leave it to professional clergy, youth ministers, authors, and others. Therefore more and more young people are left to attend to their spiritual growth without the benefit of adult mentoring during the increasingly stressful experience called adolescence.

In his book *All Grown Up and No Place To Go,* David Elkind maintains that adolescence today is an experience that puts an entire generation at risk. He describes traditional "markers" of the passage from childhood to adolescence. For example, we—the parents of today's teenagers—had to be a certain age before we found out about our family's financial state, the skeletons in our family closet, the political climate of a developing country, or the latest Wall Street index. According to Elkind, these "information markers" were subtle signals that one was moving past childhood and into the age of adolescence. In the same vein, we had to be a certain age before we could attend a dance unchaperoned, play on an athletic team with a coach and real uniforms, go across town on one's own, stay up late, or have friends spend the night. Once we experienced these "entertainment markers," we unconsciously began to feel as though we were growing up.

Elkind points out that we had to wait until we were a certain age before we could spend money at our own discretion ("purchasing markers") or wear a certain dress, get our ears pierced, use makeup, wear a sports coat, and so on ("appearance markers"). We had to be a certain age before we could date or sit with visiting adults for the duration of the visit ("social markers").

All of these information, entertainment, purchasing, appearance, and social markers indicated that one had entered into adolescence—or even just "the high school years." Today, however, these markers are being accessed by sixth-, seventh-, and eighth-graders. When high school youth see that preadolescent siblings and schoolmates wear, know, buy, view, and do the same things they do, they quickly leave traditional adolescence and engage in adult markers of entertainment, purchasing, employment, relationships, socialization, and intoxication.[5] Engaging in these markers of adulthood while lacking the necessary experience, skills, and cognitive ability puts both high school youth and early adolescents at risk.[6]

Aside from this dangerous dance of early access, the experience of childhood itself is unprecedented. Here is a list of elements from today's childhood that were never a part of childhood for previous generations, including those of us who parent today's adolescents: e-mail, the Internet, call waiting, MTV, WWF, wine coolers, tattoos, global warming, metal detectors in schools, beepers, cell phones, body piercing, high-priced athletic shoes, latch-key kids, AIDS, and CD and DVD players.

Adults who parent, counsel, teach, and minister to today's adolescents would do well to recognize and admit that we were never their age. No adult has had the kind of childhood experienced by today's adolescents. It is an unprecedented experience of growing up. Today's adult generation of parents and social scientists is not sure how such a childhood affects one's ability to navigate life's journey, for is too early to tell.

Should we then abdicate our role to parent, teach, coach, challenge, and mentor? Of course not. But it is helpful to recognize the complexity of growing up today and the corresponding need to be an intrusive presence in the lives of young people.

Fred Hechinger, author of *Fateful Choices: Healthy Youth for the Twenty-First Century,* examines in detail the issues facing adolescents as presented by the Carnegie Council on Adolescent Development. The results of this study lead to the conviction that to be and remain healthy, adolescents need the following:

- Information: a healthy education; life skills training, with special attention to decision making and conflict resolution; positive support by the media
- Access to health services: school-linked adolescent health centers; full insurance coverage, including preventative health care
- Motivation and support of adults: willingness and ability to use available information and services, especially those provided by family, youth organizations, mentors, and constructive role models
- An improved environment: reduction of poverty; control of substance abuse and guns; more effective links to the world of work[7]

In 1997 the United States government, led by Colin Powell, developed a national strategy to address a generation of youth at risk. The plan, entitled America's Promise, pinpoints essential resources for youth.

Young people today face serious threats to their futures—and even to their lives. Our goal is to mobilize as many individuals, educational and religious organizations, and small companies and large corporations to make voluntary, concrete commitments of goods, services, or funding needed to make life better for all young people. There are five critical resources that our young people must have access to if they are to thrive:

- An ongoing relationship with a caring adult: mentor, tutor, coach Safe places and structured activities during non-school hours for learning and growing
- A healthy start
- A marketable skill through effective education
- An opportunity to give back through community service

Access to one of these resources in isolation is not enough; in order to grow, young people need access to all five.[8]

Such studies and recommendations provide concrete direction and excellent approaches that serve as a rallying point for our efforts on behalf of young people.

This book, however, is grounded in the belief that the crisis facing young people includes a *crisis of the spirit* that is not addressed in America's Promise or other such efforts. The adolescent crisis of the spirit leaves young people lacking hope and feeling powerless in the face of overwhelming challenges. The crisis of the spirit is a low level of moral courage and of joy. Spiritual growth increases hope, connects one to a higher power, generates fortitude, and opens one to joy.

Recent national programs call youth-serving agencies, institutions, and adults to be an intrusive presence among young people. The approach, described in the following pages, is built on the conviction that such a presence is an *active presence* that involves checking in on adolescents, standing up for them, challenging them to be accountable, giving them a second chance, sitting quietly with them, and constantly being at the doorway to their heart and soul. It further involves waiting for an invitation to enter into their spiritual walk and, at the same time, helping them voice their deepest questions, beliefs, dreams, fears, joys, convictions, and spiritual hungers. Even though these are complicated times in society and in the lives of adolescents, this book will offer specific ways of intentionally maintaining such an intrusive presence for the purpose of fostering spiritual growth, without being an obtrusive, oppressive, or awkward presence.

Adolescent Spiritual Growth

One point stands at the core of the literature regarding the understanding of adolescent spiritual growth—adolescence itself.

Each adolescent may have a different answer to questions such as, "When have you felt closest to God in the last six months?" and "What word best describes God for you?" We will limit our ability to walk the spiritual path with adolescents if we expect young people to mirror our own experience or image of God.

Young people can articulate how they relate to God, their dominant image of God, and how God expects them to treat others. Yet adolescents change in their experience of and relationship with God— often within a span of time as short as a school year. Because adolescents often criticize the way things are, it is only natural that their spirituality involves varying degrees of criticism toward some religious doctrine and worship practices.

However the adolescent challenge to make sense of things and to find meaning in the ironies of life results in a strong and natural desire for a spirituality that touches almost all the aspects of an adolescent's life.[9] Adolescents possess a spirituality that touches the athletic field, preparation for exams, the grieving over a tragic death, the stress of problem-solving, the fear of rejection, the pain of failure, and the joy of dreams fulfilled.

As mentioned earlier, developmental views of spirituality are debatable and may be incomplete. Therefore it is helpful to remember not only the *adolescent* nature of a young person's spirituality but also its fundamental *characteristics* of adolescent spirituality—friendship, prayer, mystery, doubt, and gratitude.

Friendship is the key aspect of an adolescent's relationship to God. Although young people may relate to God as Creator, Father, Protector, and so on, each relationship includes the image of God as friend. According to Charles Shelton, author of *Adolescent Spirituality: Pastoral Ministry for High School & College Youth*:

> *It is during adolescence that God can be symbolized as a personal friend who can offer the young person a deepening relationship based on openness and trust. . . . A friendship model in the*

adolescent's relationship with the Lord seeks to touch the deepest yearnings of the adolescent's desires and dreams, to speak of the adolescent's need for closeness, understanding, intensity, security, and growth.[10]

Prayer plays a central role in the spirituality of adolescents in that it maintains the adolescent's relationship with God. Prayer involves solitude. Recently, while conducting video-taped interviews with adolescents on the topic of prayer, I was told by young people that they pray in the solitude of their bedrooms, often with their music on or the door closed. They pray under the covers before giving way to sleep. Young people pray in the solitude of walking the neighborhood, waiting for the morning school bus, practicing an athletic skill, tinkering with a project, and even sitting in a classroom among peers. In *Out Of Solitude,* Henri Nouwen describes the importance of solitude:

In solitude we can slowly unmask the illusion of our possessiveness and discover in the center of our own self that we are not what we can conquer, but what is given to us. In solitude we can listen to the voice of him who spoke to us before we could speak a word, who healed us before we could make any gesture to help, who set us free long before we could free others, and who loved us long before we could give love to anyone.[11]

Mystery is an inescapable constant within adolescent spirituality. First of all, the God adolescents relate to is a mystery. Then, as young people pray, their reflections deepen in accordance with their new experiences, discoveries, confusions, and questions. The developmental psychologists point out that adolescents' natural desire to make sense of life, coupled with their increased ability to think abstractly, brings them face-to-face with mystery regarding aspects of creation, traumatic events, the cycles of life, the existence of evil, and the struggle for justice in the world.[12]

Doubt plays a creative role within adolescent spirituality. Since criticizing is a characteristic trait of adolescence, it naturally moves young people to doubt certain religious teachings and concepts, even regarding some of the mysteries of their faith. Critical thinking, combined with a need for independence, results in spiritual doubting among adolescents. If handled well by the adult community, such doubting can result in a system of religious beliefs and moral values that the adolescent "owns" and is willing to defend, even in the face of rejection from peers.[13]

Gratitude is also a constant characteristic of adolescent spirituality. However there is a diversity and uniqueness about how and for what young people express gratitude. Adolescents are grateful to the God they relate to for protection, life, friends, parents, opportunities, and basic essentials. Yet the degree to which gratitude is an operative factor in an adolescent's spirituality varies. Adolescent preoccupation with the evolving self actually works against the gratitude element of their spirituality. Nevertheless it is an aspect of adolescent spirituality that can facilitate growth when intentionally addressed or "taught to" by caring adults. Gratitude can impact empathy, which experts tell us is a key factor in adolescent morality.[14]

Much more can be said about the nature of the adolescent's relationship to God. Nevertheless, as adults, we can begin to understand and become more confident in relating to an adolescent's spiritual life by remembering the "five fingers" working in the young soul: friendship with God, the practice of prayer, inescapable mystery, occasional doubt, and heartfelt gratitude.

Three Dimensions of Spiritual Growth

I have found it very helpful to view spirituality as consisting of three distinct yet related dimensions—religious faith, moral living, and emotional awareness. In research conducted over a three-month period with two hundred high school students, statistical analysis of students' before-and-after self-assessments indicated that the dimensions of religious faith, moral living, and emotional awareness are distinct from one another but are also interrelated.[15]

Religious Faith

Throughout history, humanity has maintained that religious faith shapes the way people "see" the God above us, within ourselves, and inside others. Today young people have a spiritual hunger and long to "see" through the eyes of faith. Therefore prayer is not perceived as something merely quaint but as the deepest source of strength and comfort; those who are poor are not seen as irresponsible but as family; and religious practices are seen as concrete ways of participating in one's relationship with God and God's people.

Faith is much more than belief. Noted religious educator Sara Little (1983) writes that "First of all, faith *is* the religiously important category, and it is not the same thing as belief. It would be hard to find anyone to quarrel with that statement."[16] Wilfred Cantwell Smith points out that there is "monstrous confusion" around the notion that belief is the same as faith.[17]

Thomas Groome, author of *Christian Religious Education: Sharing Our Story and Vision,* maintains that there are three dimensions of faith: faith as believing, faith as trusting, and faith as doing. The "believing" dimension of faith is the aspect that contains conviction. The "trusting" dimension of faith enables us to build a personal relationship with God, a relationship characterized with love, attachment, dependency, direction, awe, friendship, and so on. Faith as "trusting" represents the mutual loyalty established between humans and the Creator. The "doing" dimension of faith reflects the carrying out of God's will. It is in this dimension that one lives out God's desired engagement in the world. This dimension embodies response to the God one believes in and trusts.[18]

Given these different dimensions of religious faith, does adolescent faith have a certain emphasis? Researchers Peter Benson, Dorothy Williams, and Arthur Johnson of the Search Institute in Minneapolis, Minnesota, conducted an extensive survey of 8,165 early adolescents and their parents, through which they explored religious faith according to four different terms: *liberating, restrictive, vertical,* and *horizontal.* This research, described in their book *The Quicksilver Years: The Hopes and Fears of Early Adolescence,* points out that young people with a liberating style of religious faith emphasize the fact that God accepts them just as they are and that salvation is a gift and not something earned. They agree most strongly with statements such as, "My religious faith makes me feel as if a burden has been lifted from my shoulders" and "I know God loves me just as I am." Their dominant belief is in God's unconditional love.

Young people with a restrictive faith emphasize God's guidelines and see the doing dimension of faith as consisting of discipline, control, and limits. They agree most strongly with statements such as, "If I do a lot of wrong things, God will stop loving me," "I believe God has a lot of rules about how people should live their lives," "I believe God is very strict," and "I believe God will punish me if I do something wrong."

The vertical and horizontal dimensions of religious faith have to do with how an adolescent interprets his or her response to the God one believes in and trusts. In Groome's language, the horizontal and vertical aspects represent the direction of the "doing" dimension of faith. Adolescents with a highly vertical style of faith work on improving their personal relationship with God "above" through a practice of prayer, worship, and reading of the Scriptures. Adolescents with a highly horizontal style are most interested in caring for other people and practicing fairness, charity, and justice. To these young people, faith is far more a matter of living a loving life than deepening their personal relationship with God.

Benson and his colleagues found the following:

These four themes come in different combinations. Some people demonstrate a strong emphasis on only one dimension—a horizontal orientation, for example, that becomes visible in the life of a person who is constantly reaching out, taking care of others. Some show strong emphasis on two of them—perhaps showing a sense of religion as restricting and a vertical orientation, which would lead to careful attention to rules and limits and a private kind of religion that does not frequently include actions demonstrating care for others.[19]

I sometimes see the extremely liberating style of faith surface when I offer adolescents moral dilemmas to which, after much thought and discussion, they say things such as, "You do whatever you've got to do. God will forgive you." Young people with extremely liberating faith will tend to make statements such as, "God and I are very tight. I pray every night, especially when I'm in a bind." Yet that same young person is actively engaged in premarital sexual activity. In the extreme, young people with a liberating style of faith wear religious medals around their necks and yet are part of a gang that promotes violence. In such cases, liberating faith overemphasizes God's love and de-emphasizes accountability.

On the other hand, I have worked with young people who have an extremely horizontal style of faith and who, therefore, tend to say things such as, "I believe in God. Like God is watching over me and stuff. But I don't like pray to God a lot or go to church much. I believe God wants me to live a loving life. My faith calls me to treat other people fairly, help them out, and be a caring person."

This understanding of religious faith according to different *dimensions* (believing, trusting, doing), *styles* (restrictive, liberating), and *directions* (vertical, horizontal) offers a framework free of developmental or sequential limits. It does not maintain that children emphasize a particular element at one age, another in middle school, and yet another element or elements in adolescence. Nor does this understanding of faith propose a sequence wherein one element of faith must precede or follow another. Instead it remains open to the effects of one's upbringing and formation within the context of family, congregation, synagogue, or mosque.[20]

One last word about religious faith is necessary. Research indicates that the baby boomers and other parents who teach, coach, counsel, and care for today's adolescents understand the term *religious* in a narrower way than the one just described. Wade Roof, in his book *A Generation of Seekers: The Spiritual Journeys of the Baby Boom Generation,* reports the following:

> *The rising concern for spirituality and new imageries of the divine are shifts in religious vocabularies. Almost all of the people we talked to had an opinion about the differences between being "religious" and being "spiritual." While they did not always agree as to what the difference was, they were sure there was one. The two realms have become disjointed, according to the majority of our respondents. To be religious conveys an institutional connotation: to attend worship services, to go to Mass, to light Hanukkah candles. To be spiritual, in contrast, is more personal and empowering, and has to do with the deepest motivations in life.[21]*

The term *religious* is used by some to refer to faith as believing and trusting with a strong vertical direction (between me and God). For our purposes I also will refer to religious faith as the way people establish, strengthen, and express their personal relationship with God. This vertical relationship can be nurtured in a variety of ways, both personal and through participation in one's faith community.

However, in order to be faithful to a broader view of religious faith, we will define *spirituality* as being made up of the *vertical* dimension of religious faith, the *internal* dimension of emotional awareness, and the *horizontal* dimension of moral living.

Emotional Awareness

The role of emotions has long been an important consideration when regarding the human challenge of living a moral life. However, the theories of moral development proposed by Piaget, Kohlberg, Fowler, and others excluded the intrinsic role of emotions and have resulted in modern approaches to moral education that emphasize cognitive ability.

Moral theologians such as Jesuit Charles Shelton, moral theorists such as Alasdair MacIntyre, Norma Haan, and William Damon,[22] and character educators such as Thomas Lickona, urge us to return our attention to the role emotions play in the moral life.

Today psychologists, child-care specialists, and teachers who see a relationship between one's ability to manage emotions and one's ability to demonstrate responsible behavior challenge us to invest intentionally in the emotional dimension of our lives. The link between the two lies in what is called *emotional intelligence.*

Talk of emotional intelligence has swept the country. Yale psychologist Peter Salovey and John Mayer of the University of New Hampshire first coined the term in 1990.[23] Daniel Goleman's book *Emotional Intelligence: Why It Can Matter More than IQ* maintains that we can intentionally increase our emotional intelligence by practicing certain skills and techniques.[24] Studies such as the Penn Prevention Project, described in the book by Martin E. Seligman entitled *The Optimistic Child,* indicate that youth can be taught how to develop and employ optimistic thinking, which turns out to have a measurable and prolonged impact on self-reliance, school performance, resiliency, and physical health.[25]

For those concerned about spiritual growth, there is a strong reason and a specific purpose in teaching young people how to handle their emotions.

When I discussed the connection between emotional awareness and spiritual growth with Dr. Robert Coles, noted Harvard child psychiatrist and author, Coles asked:

> *For what?! Teach emotional awareness for what?! Most of the saints probably didn't have this "emotional intelligence," and thank God they didn't. Why, most of the saints probably would have been sent to mental hospitals. And probably by people just like me with our degrees in this or that! Emotional intelligence for what?! For the moral life, that's what! That's the only reason any of this stuff is worth it.[26]*

Aristotle also articulated the connection between virtue and emotions:

> *I speak of moral virtue, as it is moral virtue which is concerned with emotions and actions, and it is these which admit of excess and deficiency and the mean. Thus it is possible to go too far, or not to go far enough, in respect of fear, courage, desire, anger, pity, and pleasure and pain generally, and the excess and the deficiency are alike wrong; but to experience these emotions at the right times and on the right occasions and towards the right persons and for the right causes and in the right manner is the mean or the supreme good, which is characteristic of virtue.[27]*

When we see young people shooting each other in school, jumping in bed, or suffering from depression, we often think they need more religious experiences or moral teachings. But no one is more emotional than adolescents. It is their nature. It is the way God made them. What we must also see is that they need help handling their emotions.

Young people have religious faith, which experience and research confirms for us. Studies show us that young people also have a strong moral code. Yet they struggle to do what they believe is right. They struggle, like all of us, to live out the morality of their religious beliefs. In this new millennium let us offer them a spirituality that *includes* skills for emotional awareness. Such a spirituality will enable them to cope successfully with the unprecedented struggles of contemporary adolescence so that they can live the moral life and contribute to the common good.

Moral Living

The Greeks asked, "Can virtue be taught?" Socrates believed that bringing someone to the consciousness of truth, beauty, and justice would lead to a virtuous life. Plato used his "Allegory of the Cave" to stress that reasoning and intellect reveal truth that leads to virtue.

Today society is asking the same question with a new sense of urgency. The approach offered in this book reflects the belief that virtues can be taught by showing young people how to practice virtues in both normal and difficult situations and how to live the moral life as a person of conscience, character, and contribution.

Discussion has been varied regarding the degree to which females and males approach morality differently. However, empirical studies conducted by Nona Lyons and others show that there is no significant gender difference in the ethic of care among young people.[28] This undifferentiated view of morality holds that both genders have a strong desire to do good and care for others.

Much research and theory surrounds moral development, ranging from that which suggests clear moral stages and phases to that which suggests environment and culture. William Damon, in his book *The Moral Child: Nurturing Children's Natural Moral Growth*, writes:

The conceptions currently "at large" in the public purview consist of myths based either on religious or political biases or on obsolete psychological theorizing. . . . Many of our popular myths about children's moral development have been around, in one form or another, for a long time. Not surprisingly, they tend to contradict one another, for they arise from distinct competing views about human nature. Here are some of the more prevalent myths that one might encounter through public discourse and media presentations:

1. Children are naturally good but become morally corrupted when exposed to the wrong social influences.

2. Children are born with predominantly immoral tendencies, and moral sensibilities must be imposed upon them against their will from the outside.

3. The parent is solely responsible for the child's moral character.

4. There is little that anyone can do about the child's moral character, since the child's personality is formed through congenital factors that are largely beyond anyone's control.

5. Children's peers are a deleterious influence on their moral judgment and conduct.

6. For the sake of their moral growth, children need to be shielded from television, film, or music performances that suggest poor moral values.

7. Moral education means telling children about the values held by our society and the virtues expected of them.[29]

Damon maintains that these notions funnel adult efforts into fruitless and counterproductive directions that prevent us from taking "the direct, informed steps that could make a difference for our children's lives." Damon offers the following cohesive principles gleaned from scientific studies:

1. Moral awareness comes from "within" a child's normal social experience. Simply through their participation in essential social relationships, children encounter the classic moral issues facing humans everywhere: issues of fairness, honesty, responsibility, kindness, and obedience.

2. The child's moral awareness is shaped and supported by natural emotional reactions to observations and events. These emotions can be quite intense in both positive and negative ways.

3. Relations with parents, teachers, and other adults introduce the child to important social standards, rules, and conventions that provide knowledge and respect for the social order. *Authoritative* adult-child relations, in which firm demands are matched by clear communication between the adult and child about the nature and justification of these demands, yield the most positive results. Authoritative relations are very different from authoritarian or overly permissive child-rearing.

4. In peer relations children develop new procedures for interacting with others, some of which may endure into adulthood. Moreover,

the perspective-taking skills required in peer relations enhance the child's growing moral awareness and helping behaviors.

5. Because children's morality is shaped (though not wholly created) through social influence, there are broad differences among young people's moral orientations. On the other hand, children universally appreciate moral values such as truth, human rights, human welfare, and justice. These are often referred to as "natural moral values."

6. Children acquire moral values in a school setting by fully and actively participating in the adult-child and child-child relationships that support, enhance, and guide their natural moral inclinations. In order to create contexts for children's full participation in moral learning, adults must practice a *respectful engagement* with the child, in which clear adult guidance is provided after the adult productively engages the child by respecting his or her initiatives and reactions.[30]

In this chapter we have looked at how faith-filled adults have offered different theories, facts, and approaches on how to "fish the river" of adolescent spiritual growth. In the next four chapters, we will explore four intentional activities: attending to stories, building skills, honoring the senses, and offering solidarity. These four activities will allow us to access the spiritual journey of youth and will provide a way for adolescents themselves to enter more fully into the religious, moral, and emotional dimensions of their own spirituality. Maybe—just maybe—we can learn to "fish the river" of adolescent spiritual growth in a way that will lead young people to fish the river of spirituality for themselves.

FOR REFLECTION

1. Perhaps it would be fruitful to spend time reflecting on the two different ways of "fishing the river" with some questions:

   If the river symbolizes life, how do you currently fish it?

   If the river symbolizes relationships, how do you currently fish it?

   If the river symbolizes career, how do you currently fish it?

   If the river symbolizes parenting, how do you, or did you, fish it?

   If the river symbolizes your spiritual growth, how do you currently fish it?

2. "We were never their age." How much does this statement surprise you? How much do you agree with it? To what extent might it influence the way you work with adolescents?

3. If adolescent spirituality involves friendship with God, prayer, mystery, doubt, and gratitude, which element have you noticed most in the adolescent(s) for whom you care?

4. Which element do you remember most about your own spirituality during adolescence?

5. What are your thoughts about the three-dimensional view of spirituality, involving religious faith, moral living, and emotional awareness? To what degree do you find yourself agreeing or disagreeing with this view?

6. Which dimension do you think is dominant in the adolescent(s) for whom you care?

7. Which dimension is strongest in your own spirituality?

PRACTICALLY SPEAKING

- If you intentionally pay attention to the spiritual interests, questions, beliefs, and doubts of the youth with whom you work, you will be able to glimpse the dominant dimension(s) of their spirituality. Affirm the dimension(s) you recognize, and set out to intentionally nurture those that are less developed.

- Address the religious, or vertical, dimension of spirituality by sharing beliefs about God, various religious traditions, mystery, prayer rituals, and holy days as well as religious questions and uncertainties.
- Address the moral, or horizontal, dimension by debating the morality of different current events, issues of justice, school events, peer interactions, sexually explicit media, and social practices.
- Address the emotional, or internal, dimension by discussing the spiritual nature of hope, despair, powerlessness, loneliness, joy, love, anger, self-fulfillment, fear, confidence, gratitude, and so on as *experienced* by the youth with whom you work.
- If you cannot determine the dominant dimensions of a young person's spirituality, then intentionally set out to nurture each of the three different dimensions for a specific amount of time.

Chapter 2

Attending to Stories

The stories people tell have a way of taking care of them. If stories come to you, care for them. And learn to give them away where they are needed. Sometimes a person needs a story more than food to stay alive. That is why we put these stories in each other's memory. This is how people care for themselves.

Barry Lopez[1]

Stories are teaching tools that can be used to engage young people of all ages in exploring virtues, morals, character, and spirituality. Stories have been used throughout history to make a point, reveal a truth, or promote a certain behavior. A search of recent literature indicates continued interest in teaching with stories.

American educators in the nineteenth century placed emphasis on using stories. Textbooks consisted largely of stories, poetry, editorials, essays, and travel accounts that addressed the moral issues of the day. In fact, research has shown that the pedagogy of the nineteenth century relied on stories to teach academic subjects, cognitive skills, and morals.[2] Today there is a renewed call to teach with stories. Librarians, school administrators, social commentators, educators, theologians, and mental health professionals are expressing an urgent return to teaching with stories.[3]

Educators are using stories today as a means to teach math, reading, writing, problem-solving skills, and emotional awareness.[4] They are also using stories to help identify multicultural values,[5] to foster ethics in nurses,[6] and to prepare beginning teachers.[7]

Attending to stories includes stories read, written, told, and viewed on film.[8] Leland Ryken writes that "One of the most universal human impulses can be summed up in the four words: 'Tell me a story.'" He reminds us of the conclusion made by Thomas Peters and Robert Waterman in their book *In Search of Excellence* regarding the power of stories within the fabric of corporate America: "We are more influenced by stories (vignettes that are whole and make sense in themselves) than by data."[9]

The ancient Greeks asked whether virtue could be taught. Today we may reply, "Yes, with stories." Stories may be found in books, poetry, ethnic legends, movies, and television programs. These stories also may be found in the sacred scriptures of the religions of the world and in conversations that matter among family and friends.

William Bennett's *The Book of Virtues*[10] hit the best-seller list as "a treasury of great moral stories" that shed light on such virtues as responsibility, courage, compassion, loyalty, honesty, friendship, persistence, hard work, self-discipline, and faith. Elizabeth Saenger's *Exploring Ethics through Children's Literature* provides teachers with practical strategies for using stories with primary-grade students.[11] In *Books That Build Character: A Guide to Teaching Your Child Moral Values through Stories,* William Kilpatrick lists over three hundred titles of stories, biographies, sacred texts, fantasy tales, legends, and so on from a variety of different cultures.[12]

In *The Call of Stories: Teaching and the Moral Imagination,* Robert Coles describes numerous examples of how stories have been used to evoke moral issues and responses. Coles has demonstrated that children and adults can thoughtfully reflect on stories in a way that enables them to connect the content of the story to the content of their lives.[13] I, myself, have witnessed the powerful interaction between stories and students while directing the Teaching for Spiritual Growth Summer Institute with Coles. There, teachers and professional youth workers would discuss the four short stories of Tillie Olsen's *Tell Me a Riddle* and then quickly shift to related issues operative in their own lives, work, families, relationships, churches, and students.

In a similar way, the Lilly Endowment Leadership Education Program employs "depth education," in which over two thousand adult leaders come together to read stories and discuss the stories' moral issues.[14] Lawrence, Seamon, Thomas, Tirrell, and Vanderplas-Holper have all documented how children's literature, Old Testament sagas, poetry, ethnic legends, and myths have been effective as moral agents.[15]

The use of stories in moral development has captured the interest of psychologists, who have revisited this ancient teaching practice and have articulated new psychological and neurological reasons in support of teaching with stories. Their research suggests that the human brain and psyche are designed to attend to stories.[16]

Psychologists are also using literature as a form of counseling therapy.[17] In Massachusetts criminal offenders participated in a program entitled Changing Lives through Literature. Part of their sentence included the reading of novels and short stories, followed by small-group discussions with other offenders and a professor of English. According to literature professor Robert Waxler, who started the program, "There is something magical that happens around that table. It's a discussion that allows everyone involved to be reflective about the characters in the stories and about themselves."[18]

Waxler assigned male offenders such stories as *Greasy Lake* by T. Coraghessan Boyle, *Old Man and the Sea* by Ernest Hemingway, *The Sea-Wolf* by Jack London, *Of Mice and Men* by John Steinbeck, *Deliverance* by James Dickey, and *Affliction* by Russell Banks.

Professor Jean Trounstrine assigned female offenders *The Wife's Story* by Ursula LeGuin, *Dinner at the Homesick Restaurant* by Anne Tyler, *The Bluest Eye* by Toni Morrison, *Pigs in Heaven* by Barbara Kingsolver, *Their Eyes Were Watching God* by Zora Neale Hurston, *The Shipping News* by Annie Proulx, and *Tell Me a Riddle* by Tillie Olsen.

A study of the impact of Changing Lives through Literature revealed that crimes of all kinds committed by graduates dropped by 68 percent, while felony crimes dropped by almost 80 percent.[19]

Stories, like parables, can even be overtly religious. I adapted this one from Reverend Edward Hayes and have used it quite often with young people:

Angelina, a junior-high student, loved to jog. She would ride her bike to the park almost every day after school, chain it to a tree, and jog through the woods for about thirty minutes. One afternoon as she began to jog, Angelina noticed a different path through the woods. It looked less traveled and a little rough, but she decided to take a risk and took off jogging down this newly discovered path.

The path led Angelina deep into the woods, and as she jogged, her thoughts were the same as always: her day at school, boys, teachers, the upcoming basketball season, life at home, chores to be done at home, and so on. Today, however, her thoughts seemed a bit clearer on this new path filled with leaves and lined with trees swaying beautifully, clothed in the colors of fall. Because the path was not as well traveled as the other jogging path, Angelina had trouble with her footing and turned her ankle. She was in pain but hobbled over to a fallen tree and sat on it, gingerly rubbing her ankle.

From the opposite end of the path, a small figure suddenly emerged and headed toward Angelina. The person seemed to be strumming a guitar. As the figure approached, Angelina moved up the fallen tree, as far from the path as possible. The figure approached Angelina. She could hear the sound of his guitar.

He stopped and said, "Good afternoon. May I be of any assistance?"

"No, thanks. I'm fine. I turned my ankle. I'll be all right," she replied.

"Oh? Then what you need, my young friend, is some dancing music!" The musician then began playing a simple melody. When he finished, he smiled. "There. That'll do ya," he said, as he turned away and headed back down the path.

Then something strange happened to Angelina. The musician's melody filled her body and spirit. She began to dance and laugh. The pain in her ankle ceased as she twirled and skipped this little, joyful dance. She danced back along this newly found path to her bike, unchained it, and began to pedal her way back home.

She noticed a woman with a flat tire, got off her bike, danced up to the woman, and offered help. The woman just stared at Angelina dancing there on the sidewalk. Declining her help, she asked, "Are you on drugs?"

Angelina continued pedaling her way back home. When she noticed a "Help Wanted" sign outside the neighborhood grocery store, she danced into the store and inquired about the job. The manager quietly watched her dance and then replied: "Miss, I'm sorry, but feet are needed for work around here, not for dancing. Come back when you are older, and then you will understand."

So it went for Angelina. She danced all the time, even though most people didn't understand it. Her parents thought she was too noisy in her room upstairs. Her brother and sister simply thought she was being silly. Whenever classmates asked her why she kept dancing, she would say, "I don't know. It makes me feel so peaceful. Sometimes I can't help it. I think that maybe God wants me to help teach others to dance."

After about a week, Angelina no longer heard the music, and the feet that carried on her happy little dance could manage only a slow, tired shuffle. Each day she walked past the church on her way home from school. One day, feeling very tired, she shuffled her way into the church and sat in the last row. She held her head in her hands, staring at her painful feet and occasionally looking up at the Christ figure on the large cross in the front of the church. She continued to stare first at her feet and then at the large cross as she prayed. Then something very strange happened.

The Christ figure came off the large cross and began to untie her shoes, humming the exact same song she had heard the musician playing in the woods. Once again the music filled her body. She and the Christ figure began to dance. They laughed and twirled together. Angelina loved it! She said softly to herself, "Now I know what it really means to be religious!" The dancing was wonderful. But suddenly things began to fade. She started to hear voices yelling. They got stronger as the Christ figure and the melody slipped away.

The voices woke her up. It was Saturday morning and her brother and sister were having a fight over the TV. It had all been a dream. She sat upright in bed and yelled at the ceiling, "It was real! It was real! It had to be real!"

She and her family went to Church that evening, as was their custom, but Angelina was in a daze. She could not remember standing, sitting, or singing during the service. Instead, she simply stared at the Christ figure on the large cross at the front of the church and thought about her dream . . . or whatever it was.

After the service, she told her parents that she wanted to talk to somebody and would return home by herself. Angelina noticed the congregation's youth minister, pastor, and a teacher she liked standing at the front of the church. She decided to take a risk and said to them, "I have to tell you about this dream I had." She described the entire dream but spent most of her time explaining what it had taught her about what it means to be religious. When she had finished explaining everything she learned about the true meaning of being religious, the youth *minister, pastor, and, teacher smiled. Then one of them said, "Dream or no dream, we have believed for a long time what you have learned about really being religious."*[20]

This story evokes wonderful discussion among young people (and adults) when followed by the simple question, "What did Angelina discover about what it really means to be religious?" I often have groups process this story by making a list under the heading "Being Religious."

All of this suggests that the question no longer is, "Can virtues be taught?" nor "Can stories teach virtues?" Now the question is, "How can interested adults use stories to glimpse and nurture the spiritual lives of adolescents?"

Story Themes for Spiritual Growth

Are there specific themes in stories that can evoke spiritual reflection among adolescents?

The twentieth-century monk Thomas Merton, known for the impact his writings had on the enhancement of spirituality in the United States, was also one of the century's most convincing voices regarding the integration of religion and literature.[21] Michael Barnes, among others, echoes the power of stories:

> *Our way of telling stories keeps reinterpreting to us who we are and who we should now become. It is a little frightening to be so responsible for our own vision of life. But a good standard to guide us in this work may be that of fidelity to what God apparently has made us capable of being, the storytellers whose stories affect one another's loves. The stories that teach us to care for one another as persons, as imaginative and free and responsible and loving persons, would be good stories for Christians to tell. The stories that remind us that we are limited beings finding our relation to the unlimited God partly through our imaginative storytellers would be stories both deeply human and deeply religious.*[22]

Catherine Madsen suggests one particular theme when she writes that:

> *The tales we care for lastingly are the ones that touch on the redemptive. . . . It is a singular idea . . . that insists on the freedom to change one's life.*[23]

Each summer from 1993 through 1998, a different group of exemplary private and public school teachers, administrators, and professional youth ministers from approximately fifteen different states were invited to Boston to participate in a ten-day discussion on teaching for spiritual growth. Led by Dr. Robert Coles and myself, the Teaching for Spiritual Growth Summer Institute began in 1993 at the Weston Jesuit School of Theology in Cambridge, Massachusetts. Sponsored by a grant from Foundations and Donors Interested in Catholic Activities (FADICA), we would discuss questions such as:

How do children and youth understand and make meaning of the religious traditions into which they are born?

What influences do family, culture, and circumstances have on spirituality?

What factors stimulate the spiritual journey of children and youth?

Can spirituality impact life?

What teaching skills are most helpful in facilitating the spiritual growth of children and youth?

What are the specific issues and challenges involved in facilitating spiritual growth among economically disadvantaged and/or at-risk youth?

What new teaching initiatives can enhance the faith life of students?

I recently conducted a qualitative analysis of the comments made by over one hundred teachers and youth workers during those five Teaching For Spiritual Growth Summer Institutes. Their comments suggest that when any form of story deals with specific themes, it can evoke true spiritual reflection and conversation. The following list contains some of these story themes for spiritual growth.

- Confession
- Loss
- Vulnerability
- Labeling
- Blindness
- Hope
- Power
- Fear
- Making meaning
- Redemption
- Evil
- Aspirations
- Pain
- Fierce determination
- Imagination
- Commitment

- The sacred
- Resiliency
- The system
- Hypocrisy
- Drunkenness
- Anger
- Failure
- Intimacy
- Self-doubt
- Death
- Afterlife
- Angels unaware
- Discipleship
- The moral life
- Questioning
- Expectations

Vigen Guroian lists similar themes in *Tending the Heart of Virtue: How Classic Stories Awaken a Child's Moral Imagination* and offers numerous examples of the power of stories to evoke the moral imagination of the readers:

> *We need desperately to adopt forms of moral pedagogy that are faithful to the ancient and true vocation of the teacher—to make persons into mature and whole human beings, able to stand face to face with the truth about themselves and others, while desiring to correct their faults and emulate goodness and truth wherever it is found. We need to take greater advantage of the power in stories to humanize the young. . . .* [24]

There is new research regarding the use of narrative among minority groups.[25] Familiarity with the issues a certain group is struggling with can lead to more insightful selection of evocative stories. For example, research has shown that the task of spiritual formation through stories within the African American culture has to do with the fostering of hope. It is this theme of hope that integrates cultural proverbs and symbolic conversations with God into a critical reflection on stories exploring hopeful and creative life choices.[26]

However, there must be careful examination of cultural and gender stereotyping in the use of stories for spiritual growth. Traditional moral stories tend to view the male as hero and the female as needy or morally disengaged.[27]

Some Research on Gender Differences

The issue of stereotyping leads to questions related to gender differences in the development and understanding of ethics:

Do females approach ethics differently than males?

How valid is the theory that males operate out of an ethic of justice while females operate out of an ethic of care?

If this theory is valid, will stories evoke different responses from young people, depending on their gender?

In 1982, Carol Gilligan identified "a different voice" inherent to the feminine approach to ethics that was not the same as the masculine approach previously reported by Lawrence Kohlberg and others.[28] Since then, ethicists, moralists, psychologists, theologians, and religious educators have supported the notion of gender differences regarding one's approach to ethics.

Gender-differentiated views of ethics uphold the premise that males have an ethic of justice while females have an ethic of care. This is Gilligan's premise of "a different voice." Gilligan believes that the work of Kohlberg places value on individualism (a male trait) and is incompatible with females because of their innate tendency to place value on community and cooperation.[29]

The view of gender differences in morality and ethics is an ancient one. Pythagoras's doctrine of reincarnation in the sixth century held that the soul of a woman was halfway between a man's and an animal's. Plato, in his fourth-century *Timaeus*, claimed that women indeed had souls but were not able to achieve the same degree of virtue as men. Women philosophers of the same era, such as Phintys of Sparta, Perictione I, and, later, Theano II, proposed a feminine morality of caring—for spouses, children, babies, servants, slaves, and self.[30]

Historically, the gender difference in ethics can be summed up in brief: males were rational while females were relational. Therefore, men were "naturally" inclined toward an ethic of logical reasoning as reflected in the law and in lives that emphasized justice. Women were naturally inclined toward an ethic of compassion as reflected in relationships and in lives that emphasized nurturing.

Is there really a gender difference in ethics? Do males operate out of an ethic of justice while females operate out of an ethic of care? Researchers and theorists have followed up Gilligan's work with new empirical studies of their own. Some of those studies are contained in *Who Cares? Theory, Research, and Educational Implications of the Ethic of Care.*[31]

Bill Puka in chapter 2 of *Who Cares?* points out several limits to Gilligan's research: She does not observe moral or ethical development over time and only conceptualizes how one level of care might build upon another. She does not trace the transition from one level to another so as to show the transformation process she predicts. She does not provide critical distinctions among socialization, consciousness-raising, and cognitive development. In addition, some of the key features of each level disappear from the sequence as one moves from one level to another.[32]

Carlene Haddock Seigfried sees a different problem with Gilligan's theory of "a different voice." She has

> ... *serious reservations about the value of research which reinforces the stereotypical association of "care" with women and "justice" with men, rather than investigating the constellation of factors which has given rise to this stereotype and its impact on women's and men's gender identities and social situations.*

Seigfried goes on to state that she rejects "biological reductionism and its psychological corollaries," and she attributes gender differences, like all other interesting human variations, to an individually creative response.[33] In short, Seigfried supports nurture's interacting with nature instead of the dominant role of "nature" as found in the gender-difference theories of ethics.

Perhaps a gender-difference theory of ethics can make the case that women have an ethic of care different from men's ethic of justice because of the *context* of their lives. After all, it is commonly agreed that young boys and young girls are socialized to be different. John Dewey, in *Context and Thought,* argues that "neglect of context is the greatest single disaster which philosophic thinking can incur."[34]

Mary Pipher presents a compelling view of the harmful effects of American socialization on adolescent girls in *Reviving Ophelia.*[35] Nel Noddings points to the social context of women and their relationships, proposing that the basic question of ethics is, "How am I to meet the other morally?" The answer she offers is that one must meet the other as one.[36] Yet we are left with an empirical question: "Do females and males actually differ in their approach to ethics?"

The data clearly indicates that females are more *emotionally responsive* than males, but not because of any biological differences.[37] Females are more emotionally responsive because of social cognition—the result of socialization rather than because of genetics or neurology.[38] Research has shown that *there are no gender differences regarding empathy.*[39] There is little to support the popular correlation between the degree of emotional responsiveness and the degree of empathy.

Recent studies reveal that males and females do not differ markedly in their reasoning on Kohlberg's moral dilemmas.[40] Eisenberg, Fabes, and Shea report that their studies seem to indicate that the differences "generally have not been large" and conclude that we must "examine factors that account for *individual differences*" in these types of responses from males and from females.[41]

Bebeau and Brabeck report that "To date, the literature examining gender differences in moral reasoning as defined by Kohlberg's theory does not support Gilligan's claim."[42] Baumrind reported that when the effects of education are controlled, indications of gender differences are totally absent.[43]

Meta-analysis by Thoma found that education was 500 times more powerful than gender in predicting moral judgment.[44]

According to Bebeau and Brabeck, "These results indicate that females use concepts of justice in making moral judgments as often as their male counterparts."[45]

It appears from the research that the question of gender differences in ethics calls for further study. However, much has been learned since Carol Gilligan first raised the question in 1982:

1. There is an ethic of care that is different from an ethic of justice. The ethic of care emphasizes the centrality of relationships and community. The ethic of justice emphasizes the centrality of rationale and legal principles.

2. There are gender differences regarding emotional responsiveness. Females display a higher degree of emotional responsivity than males. This difference is due to socialization and not to genetics.

3. The genders do not differ in their approach to ethics and morality. The research supports an undifferentiated view of ethics.

4. Most people have both a care and a justice orientation to ethics. The differences lie in the wisdom of the ratio between care and justice that each individual or community assigns to particular situations and questions.

5. Some ethical dilemmas have proven to evoke more of an ethic of care, while other types of ethical dilemmas and questions predictably evoke an ethic of justice, regardless of one's gender.

6. Education is clearly a powerful influence on ethics of care and justice. More research on the influence of education could be of great help to those involved in character education, religious education, and counseling.

There are cultural differences in the role women play in ethical and moral leadership. African American women are regularly given this role by their communities, who bestow upon them the title "Mother."[46] Latin American women often assume the roles of advocates for ethical and moral government policies and social services.[47] It is interesting to note that these are the very same ethical titles and roles held by many feminine Christian models, such as Mary, the mother of Jesus, Hildegard of Bingen, Joan of Arc, and so on.

Using Stories in the Public Setting

As a nation concerned about its youth, we should continue exploring the role of moral and religious stories within our public education system. It is interesting to note that religion clauses begin the first amendment. It is even more helpful to remember that the first amendment begins with *two* religion clauses: "Congress shall make no law respecting the establishment of religion, *or prohibiting the free exercise thereof.*" It may be that most of the post-modern discussion has focused only on the first clause. While the framers of the Constitution were determined to ensure freedom from any government-imposed religion, they took pains to ensure the right of individuals to free exercise of religion. Gregory refers to the work of Lawrence Tribe, who in defending Pennzoil before the Supreme Court, reminded the Court of what Chief Justice Warren Burger once pointed out:

> *A pervasive difficulty in the constitutional jurisprudence of the religion clauses has accordingly been the struggle to find a neutral course between the two religion clauses, both of which are cast in absolute terms, and either of which, if expanded to logical extreme, would tend to clash with the other.*[48]

Yet the two religion clauses do not prohibit the teaching of moral values in public schools as long as the schools avoid endorsing any particular set of values at the exclusion of someone else's. No one's free exercise of religion can be fostered to the detriment of another's. If the Ten Commandments were posted in a public school classroom, which version would one see—Protestant, Catholic, or Jewish? If each version were posted, would public school teachers be able to explain the differences sufficiently? And what about the Constitutional rights of Buddhists or Muslims? If the Bible were to be read, which version would not exclude another's beliefs?

The teaching of moral values in public schools can be carried out with care and respect for the rights of all the public. There is a commonly accepted core collection of moral values befitting the human condition and the common good.

However, the teaching of moral values should not become a vehicle for the political agenda of any particular religion. In *Teaching Moral Value in the Public Schools,* Gregory warns that:

> *Those fanatics who wish to sweep aside either of the first amendment's two religion clauses should take heed from the lawyer (and Catholic saint) Sir Thomas More, whose son-in-law Roper was confused by More's releasing of an enemy because the enemy violated no law. Roper claimed he would "cut down every law in England to get at the Devil," to which More asked what would then be left to protect Roper should the Devil eventually turn and seek him out.*[49]

Conclusion

It must be noted that contemporary stories are not just found in print. Evocative stories dealing with the preceding themes are presented on film and television. This growing source of story is easily accessible to most adolescents. Using film and television to foster the spiritual growth of adolescents should be seen as an opportunity by all of us.[50] For example, I—and many others—have used Spike Lee's film *Malcolm X* with teens as a vivid story of spiritual growth. Adolescents need only a little assistance from caring adults to see beneath the sensationalized rhetoric and politics in this story and to recognize the three dimensions of religious faith, moral living, and emotional awareness that comprise Malcolm's spiritual growth and our own.

In addition, evocative stories on the themes listed earlier are found printed in the sacred writings of most religions. Such stories were told for generations before they were ever recorded. One of the tasks of formal religious education is to help adolescents gain a certain level of knowledge and religious literacy regarding the truth and wisdom of such sacred stories. For example, the Old Testament story of Joseph, which appears in both Hebrew and Christian Scripture, contains at least seven spiritual growth themes, all of which can evoke conversations about adolescent spiritual life—as can the various Gospel stories.

Evocative stories with spiritual growth themes are also lived and shared in conversations. Research indicates that learning is greater among students who share from their personal experiences than among students who participate in a common experience. This kind of experience-based learning seems more productive than experiential learning.[51]

Such stories are found in the daily experiences of each adolescent. These experiential stories are shared in conversations that occur in cars, gyms, cafeterias, driveways, and phone calls.

Biographical story-sharing, in which young people share and compare aspects of their own life stories for the presence of, or need for, virtues, morals, and spiritual growth, is a common and often spontaneous practice among adolescents and those who work with them. Theologian and storyteller John Shea writes that everyone is a storyteller and that each person's unique life history influences that person's perception of God. He maintains that stories, fables, and myths shed light on the transcendent present in everyday experiences. According to Shea:

> *The experiences of contingency, dialogue, communion, moral ambiguity, and disenchantment are a few of the paths which people travel to become aware of their relatedness to Mystery. . . . In this Mystery, the adolescent confronts what is above and beyond the self. This Mystery is ambiguous and at times fleeting, but it is the foundation for all human activity.*[52]

Here is a story from everyday human activity that I have used from time to time.

> *The mother cried when she unwrapped her present. The gift wasn't perfect, but it was true. A year earlier, her nine-year-old daughter, in helping prepare the house for company, dropped a Belleek china plate that Grandmother had brought home from her only trip to Europe and had given to the child's mother. The mother cherished this china plate, because she knew it was Nanny's way of showing her love during a time when the mother—who loved the finer things of life—could only manage to serve her children red beans and rice.*
>
> *The daughter and her mother had a strong and loving relationship. They spent hours together at Girl Scout meetings, watched movies together on rainy weekends, organized birthday parties, and cooked together.*

When the daughter dropped the cherished china plate, it shattered into pieces both large and small. The sound of the broken pieces rattling on the floor evoked a stunned silence in the house. The two brothers and the father all stared at the shattered plate with mouths and eyes wide open.

The daughter never looked down at the broken pieces. Instead, she stood straight up with her eyes fixed on her mother's.

The pain on the mother's face was obvious. Her color went from white to red to gray. For a second, her eyes welled up with tears. Then she shook off the pain and broke the silence. With her daughter's face still fixed on her, the mother embraced her and said. "That's okay, Kristen. I know you didn't mean it."

Company was coming, and the mother reminded everyone to get back to their assigned clean-up and set-up tasks. As she and the kids returned to their work in slow motion, the dad knelt down on the kitchen floor, picked up all of the pieces, and put them into a brown lunch bag. Somehow he couldn't bring himself to throw it out, so he put the bag in the bottom of his dresser drawer.

Later that evening, when the kids went to bed and the company went home, the mother and father cleaned up the dishes together and talked about the evening. Then the father told the mother how sorry he was that her favorite plate had been broken. She replied, "When I looked at Kristen's face, all I could see was the time I dropped my mother's pineapple upside-down cake for the guests that were coming over. When I dropped that cake, I knew how much it hurt my mother, but she didn't yell at me. She just held me. I never forgot how my mother handled that situation. She yelled at me a lot before and after that incident, but when I dropped that precious cake just as company was pulling into the driveway, she had the compassion to hug me. And so when Kristen dropped that plate, I knew— actually I felt—that it was my turn to hug her, even though it broke my heart to lose Mom's plate."

One Friday night, about ten months later, the father gathered the children together to discuss what gift to buy the *mother for her birthday that Sunday. Someone suggested a plate "like the one that got broken." Everyone loved the idea. They agreed to go shopping the next day for a plate. The father found the brown lunch bag in the bottom of his dresser drawer, pulled out two pieces of the broken plate, and took them along.*

They went from store to store, showing the clerks the two broken pieces in hopes of finding a replacement plate. None of the stores had anything close to the original one. "It really is an antique plate," said one clerk. "It's not in any of the catalogs," said another. Finally, near closing time, the clerk at the last store looked at the pieces of the broken plate and said, "That plate cannot be bought in the United States. You probably have to go to Europe to get it."

The family did not know what to do. Mom's birthday was tomorrow. Then someone said, "Let's glue it back together!"

They rushed home to the brown bag in the father's drawer. Piece by piece, they began to glue the plate together. Glue stuck to their fingers, causing their skin to stick to the plate. One giggled that the process would never work. Another assured the rest that it was totally impossible. Everyone said it felt like trying to figure out how to put a puzzle together.

As the plate began to reappear, the giggles increased. Finally it was all put back together. You could see all the cracks, and some little tiny pieces were missing. In fact, one part of the plate still had a tiny hole in it. But the plate, despite it's cracks, held together, and the symbol of what it stood for was loud and strong. It wasn't perfect, but it was true.

They decided to "let it sit" overnight under someone's bed. The next day the mother was presented with a gift wrapped in dish towels instead of colorful paper. She rolled her eyes at the sight of the towels and said jokingly, "This should be interesting."

When she removed the towels it took her breath away. She didn't open her mouth wide and grasp for air. Her breath came out of her the way the last bit of air comes out of an old balloon that is almost flat. She did not scream with glee. She just whispered softly, "My plate." Then she began to cry. Almost everyone else did, too. The five-year-old son, the thirteen-year-old son, and the thirty-something dad all had tears in their eyes. But not the daughter. She stared at the mother's face and beamed. It was payback time.

The one act of love, given years ago when a pineapple upside-down cake hit the floor and passed on when a china plate was broken, had birthed the act of love now being given in return. Loving acts do that.

FOR REFLECTION

1. What do you think Angelina learned about what it really means to be religious?

2. How might this be helpful to the adolescent(s) for whom you care?

3. Name a story found in print or film that still evokes religious, moral, or emotional insights for you.

4. Now review the story themes for spiritual growth listed on page 40 and see whether you can identify the one(s) most present in the evocative story you just named in question 3.

5. What other story themes do you want to add to the list?

6. What gender differences do you think really exist? How can this difference help you as you participate in the spiritual growth of adolescents?

7. Did the story of the broken plate evoke any spiritual theme for you? If so, can you name it?

PRACTICALLY SPEAKING

- It helps to identify the theme(s) of a story being discussed or shared. Then you can move the discussion from the specifics of the story to the experiences and beliefs of a young person regarding that particular theme. For example: "So, in your opinion, this movie is really about sticking up for your convictions. What message do you get about sticking with your convictions? Do you find this message to be true?"

- Do not imply right or wrong ways to understand a story.

- Ask clarifying questions to help adolescents explore their views. For example: "Are you saying _____ or are you saying _____?"

- Watch the pace. Keep the conversations moving, and don't attend to stories longer than the adolescents are willing to do so. On the other hand, don't shortchange a potentially rich conversation by allowing them to respond with superficial or overly simple comments and conclusions.

- If a young person overlooks a valuable theme in the story, then tease that theme out with a direct question, such as, "What do you think the story has to say about [identify the theme]?"
- There are several ways to open up a discussion about a story. An unstructured approach can begin with an invitational question, such as, "So, what do you understand from this story/movie/song/poem?" A more structured way of attending to a story can offer these three questions, moving from one question to the next only after the previous question has been discussed: "What did you hear or see in this story/movie/song/poem?" followed by, "What feelings did it bring out in you?" and, eventually, "Based on what you heard, saw, and felt, what thoughts or conclusions do you have?"

Chapter 3

Building Skills

I remember the exact moment I first thought about teaching adolescents skills for spiritual growth. In July 1987, I began my new job as the Director of Religious Education at Boys Town in Omaha, Nebraska. It was my second day on the job, and I was in the midst of a week-long training program for new employees who would be working directly with Boys Town's young people.

The training focused on teaching youth social skills, such as how to accept feedback, how to disagree appropriately, and how to give a greeting. These social skills are absolutely essential for the success of at-risk youth, and I have yet to find any place where they are taught as thoroughly and effectively as at Boys Town.

During a training session, I suddenly had an idea. Why not teach adolescents faith development skills? I spent the next hour furiously writing down the kind of faith development skills that were not part of the social skills curriculum. Reverend Val Peter, Executive Director of Boys Town, then helped incorporate the teaching of faith development skills into the education program. In addition, dedicated and risk-taking teachers and ministers at Boys Town combined their efforts to help secure several research grants from the Lilly Endowment in order to test and measure the impact of actually teaching adolescents skills for spiritual growth during a four-year period.

Since then, Boys Town has expanded its approach to faith development skills and the integration of social skills.[1] I, myself, went on to spend six of the next nine years designing, testing, and measuring more and more skills for spiritual growth with mainstream adolescents and also integrating new findings of those working with youth on virtues in character education, multiple intelligences, the development of empathy, models of student assessment, resiliency, and service.

My work and research have convinced me that building skills for spiritual growth with adolescents is not an activity normally conducted in our various efforts to facilitate adolescent spiritual growth and provides a missing link in the work of our churches, synagogues, youth programs, and parents. Visualize the effort we all make at fostering adolescent spiritual growth as a pie cut into four slices: knowledge, attitudes, behaviors, and skills. Think about the proportion of time we devote to helping young people grow in each of these areas. Which area receives the greatest attention? Which receives the least? Most of our efforts at facilitating adolescent spiritual growth are directed at helping students assimilate important religious knowledge and embrace certain attitudes. Smaller slices of the pie are devoted to the promotion of specific behaviors or skills.

The activity of building skills for spiritual growth *intentionally* makes skills and behaviors a well thought-out piece of the pie by increasing the amount of time spent on introducing skills, checking for understanding, and practicing skills with young people. However, the building of skills for spiritual growth is not meant to replace the traditional task of helping young people gain religious knowledge. Weakening efforts to pass on religious knowledge results in a religiously illiterate and morally confused generation. Instead, this skill-building is meant to show young people how they can *put religious knowledge into practice*. While many of our spiritual growth efforts help adolescents learn *about* something, a skills-based approach helps them learn *how to do* something.

A skills approach builds on adolescents' knowledge of the Bible by teaching them how to apply the Bible to their lives. In addition to learning about the value of prayer, a skills approach teaches students how to pray. In addition to promoting an appreciation for our moral values, a skills approach teaches adolescents how to distinguish between right and wrong. Simply put, building skills for spiritual growth consists of intentional activities that teach adolescents how to apply the spiritual knowledge and attitudes they have come to believe in and cherish.

Are there really skills for spiritual growth?

If so, can they intentionally be taught, or are they learned through relationships and experiences?

Can growth in these skills be measured?

Some Specific Examples of Skills for Spiritual Growth

Building skills for spiritual growth actually has its roots deep within the tradition of religious practices, or specific behaviors that embody the way of God. In most religions of the world, such practices, or behaviors, have always included communal worship, reading sacred Scripture, witnessing, confession and reconciliation, service, hospitality, bearing one another's burdens, and so on. In *Practicing Our Faith: A Way of Life for a Searching People,* Craig Dykstra and Dorothy Bass refer to Christian practices:

> *Christian practices are things Christian people do together over time in response to and in light of God's active presence for the life of the world. . . . Practices address fundamental human needs and conditions through concrete human acts. . . . Practices therefore have practical purposes: to heal, to shape communities, to discern. . . . Practices are done together and over time . . . a practice has a certain internal feel and momentum . . . each practice is also ever new, taking fresh form each day, as it subtly adapts to find expression in every neighborhood and land. . . . Practices possess standards of excellence. . . . Finally, when we see some of our ordinary activities as Christian practices, we come to perceive how our daily lives are all tangled up with the things God is doing in the world.[2]*

However, skills for spiritual growth are not the same as practices. Skills involve the basic tasks or components that make up the broader behavior or practice. Skills are more technical than practices. An example of a spiritual practice is suffering with others, but learning how to show empathy is an example of a *skill* related to that practice. Confession and reconciliation are examples of spiritual practices, while learning how to obtain a second chance is a related skill. It may be helpful to consider skills for spiritual growth as exercises that contribute to an adolescent's ability and willingness to demonstrate spiritual practices. Moreover, adolescents want these skills.

My colleagues and I once surveyed 1,600 high school students to determine how much they felt the need for spiritual growth skills. They were given a survey listing twenty-nine skills for spiritual growth and asked to indicate whether they thought each skill was "not needed," "needed a little," "needed," or "very needed." Of those surveyed, 76 percent of the sophomores and juniors felt that all of the twenty-nine skills listed on the survey were "very needed" or "needed" while 72 percent of the freshmen and 70 percent of the seniors felt that way for all twenty-nine skills. Seventy-seven percent of the females and nearly 73 percent of the males felt that all of the skills were "very needed" or "needed."

A program was designed to address relevant skills within the three different dimensions of spiritual growth we have already discussed: religious faith, moral living, and emotional awareness.

Religious faith skills include:
- How to recognize God's presence
- How to pray
- How to share faith experiences
- How to apply the Bible to one's own life
- How to use religious imagination
- How to participate in communal worship

Moral living skills include:
- How to handle sexual and social pressure
- How to recognize and respond to others in need
- How to build and maintain healthy relationships (and terminate unhealthy ones)
- How to obtain second chances
- How to handle violence
- How to analyze society's values and issues
- How to distinguish between right and wrong

Emotional awareness skills include:
- How to stay hopeful
- How to handle anger
- How to handle fear
- How to initiate and accept reconciliation
- How to practice problem solving
- How to express affection
- How to handle rejection

This skills-based program was then tested with two hundred adolescents in various settings. All the young people rated themselves in each of the skills at the beginning of the program and again three months later at the end of the program. Each participant completed a writing sample at the beginning and at the end of the program and also turned in written and verbal evaluations at every pilot site. All materials were anonymous. Students stapled their before-and-after self-assessments together. The two-hundred pairs of self-assessments were collected and statistically analyzed by Dr. John Convey of the Catholic University of America in Washington, D.C.[3] The results are as follows:

- The two hundred students who participated in the first draft of the program reported statistically significant growth in 90 percent of the skills (t-test).
- The before-and-after writing samples revealed that students progressed in understanding how these skills 1) help them become stronger spiritually and morally, 2) give them confidence in dealing with their emotions, and 3) enable them to make good decisions, to enjoy life, and to have hope for the future (content analysis).
- Each of the three skill areas (religious faith, moral living, and emotional awareness) are distinct and interrelated (principal axis factor analysis and varimax rotation).
- The skills contained in each of these three areas reliably measure what they are intended to measure (Cronbach's Alpha).

Since this previous research, I have expanded the skills for spiritual growth into two other skill areas: gospel living skills, which help one put into practice some of the teachings of Jesus, and forecasting skills, which help one anticipate upcoming situations and take initiative for the next step. Forecasting skills can move one out of a reactionary mode and into a productive mode.

While most of the world's religions promote certain behaviors, the activity of building skills for spiritual growth introduces young people to the specific tasks that make up those behaviors. For example, most religions encompass a theology of hope, and they share the sacred writings that provide followers with the best reasons to be hopeful. However, the activity of building skills breaks down hopefulness into specific tasks, such as showing adolescents how to stay hopeful by identifying and analyzing their thoughts when discouraging things occur. For theologies that promote forgiveness, building skills that teach adolescents how to initiate and accept reconciliation are helpful. In addition to learning about dating and friendship issues, building skills for spiritual growth helps young people learn how to demonstrate affection, how to practice empathy, and how to recognize virtues.

A theology of charity and mercy, which calls for followers to be loving and to practice nonviolence and peace (a behavior), may be furthered and enhanced by building skills that teach young people how to handle their anger. During my first attempt at teaching such skills to a group of thirty-five teens, a young woman initiated the following exchange with me and the group:

> *"Do you see this hickey on my neck?" the young woman asked the group.*
>
> *We all bent sideways to get a good look, and then we all nodded.*
>
> *"It's really a birthmark," she said.*
>
> *One sensitive boy offered consolation, "But I didn't notice it before."*
>
> *"No one ever notices it at first," she said. "Then later they do notice it and they think, 'It wasn't there yesterday.' Well, I work at a fast-food restaurant, and adults come in all the time, look at my 'hickey,' and then they make all kinds of embarrassing comments."*
>
> *She paused and then said, "I'm really angry about it." The young woman took a deep breath and concluded that "This two-step process you're teaching us isn't going to work for me."*
>
> *I nodded in agreement.*
>
> *Then another girl addressed the group, saying, "I'm sixteen, and I'm not ready to date yet." She stopped because the entire group seemed to lean forward as though they weren't sure they had heard correctly. Sensing their disbelief, she repeated, "I'm just not ready yet!"*
>
> *Then her eyes began to well up, and in a trembling voice, she said, "You should hear the kinds of things the boys say and see*

what they do to me in the hall at school. . . . And even the girls
who are my friends say hurtful things behind my back. . . . I'm
really angry about it, . . . and I don't think this process of yours
is going to work for me."
    I nodded in agreement.

That exchange highlights three things you should know about the activity of building skills for spiritual growth: 1) Young people *really* want these skills to help them survive; 2) It is sometimes necessary to try several approaches before you find one that works (I did so the next day.); and 3) The activity of building skills for spiritual growth will take you, as it has taken me, to places you have never gone before with young people—places of new conversations, greater expectations, and specific behaviors.

An Illustration

Consider the merit of rediscovering and promoting moral decision making as a Christian practice. What are the components to such a practice? Are there certain related skills?

I coach young people that the skill and the practice of moral decision making involves the process of weighing—with sincerity and authenticity in light of one's relationship with God—the wisdom of four sources: sacred writings, denominational traditions, science, and community.

However, the key to this process is to weigh all four sources of wisdom without allowing one source to negate the other. Two things may happen as a result of this process: 1) a person may find out that she or he clearly takes complete direction from one or two sources of wisdom without regard for the others, or 2) the sources of wisdom conflict with each other, and the person trying to make a moral decision may be unable to determine a clear direction.

The practice of moral decision making does not ensure moral certainty regarding each and every decision; however, the practice does ensure that one will be on the road of the moral life in terms of moral accountability.

In order to practice moral decision making, we can teach young people to apply the process described above to the specific *act, intention,* and *circumstance* of the situation at hand. For example, two teenagers have been dating for three years and now are getting ready to leave to attend different colleges. They want to engage in sexual intercourse. The practice of moral decision making invites them to consider the *act* of premarital intercourse, their *intentions* related to the act, and the *circumstances* involved.

The wisdom of their sacred writings and denominational tradition clearly defines the act as morally wrong. Science informs them of health risks and emotional risks and places the act in an objectionable light (as it would smoking or drug use). The community's wisdom varies. Pop culture portrays the act as acceptable. The adult culture sends mixed signals; some parents oppose it, while others do not. Some adult counselors urge the two teens away from the act, while others defer to the view of the teens themselves, perhaps by asking, "Do you see anything wrong with it?" Which source of wisdom means the most to these two teens?

We must remind young people to consider the morality of the act with authenticity and sincerity. What do they see? Do they see dependency, convenience, curiosity, and hormonal impulses? Or do they see an expression of their love for each other?

I also remind them to consider their relationship with God. Is it such that they believe the act to be morally acceptable ("God knows we are not taking this lightly" or "God wants me to do what I believe in my heart is right")? Or does their relationship with God cause them to see the act as morally objectionable ("I just think God would want me to save sex for marriage" or "I think God would not want me to complicate my life or take any risks")?

And what of their intentions? Would the wisdom of sacred writings and denominational traditions judge the act differently, given their intentions ("We plan on getting married" or "We want to show our love for each other")? Would the wisdom of sacred writings or denominational tradition see it differently under certain circumstances ("We will be going to different schools next year" or "One of us was depressed and lonely, in need of this kind of love")?

Then there is a case to be made about natural moral law, natural virtues, and objective morality. Some acts are morally wrong "no matter what." Is this one of those acts?

We can see that the process and practice of moral decision making gives each young person a way of sorting through the questions and navigating his or her journey through the moral life with a kind of moral compass. Each person will make moral decisions that he or she may later regret or that take one down wayward trails during the journey. Although we are all vulnerable to impulsivity, we can encourage adolescents to take a moment to think. We can encourage them to be reflective. I tell adolescents that not to engage in the practice of moral decision making is to travel through life without a moral compass or a map. Not to engage in this practice is to travel the moral journey relying only on the stars, which is of little help in stormy weather or on the cloudy days of moral grayness. Maybe, even worse, not to engage in the practice of moral decision making is not to travel at all.

While the particular activity of building skills and the general activity of promoting spiritual practices usually take place within a more formal environment of teaching and learning, they most certainly can be carried out by interested adults in informal and unstructured settings. Promoting religious practices and skills for spiritual growth is an activity that can be intentionally, yet informally, carried out by grandparents, mentors, coaches, clergy, parents, relatives, and educators.

Ways of Building Skills for Spiritual Growth

Testing and measuring the activity of building skills with adolescents has led me to conclude that interested adults can be most effective when they adopt a simple approach, go deep into the experience of the adolescent as quickly as possible, and, depending on the nature of the skill, employ three "teaching" methods.

1. Some skills, such as how to apply the Bible to your life or how to stay hopeful, are brand new to young people. With new skills, using direct instruction and pointing out the specific steps of those skills is most effective. In other words, when teaching adolescents brand new skills that are not within the fabric of their everyday experience, adults should tell the young people how to do them, check for understanding, and then provide some opportunity for practice.

2. When young people are already familiar with a skill, such as how to share faith experiences, adults can simply and clearly remind them of its value and then provide engaging practice opportunities.

3. Sometimes a skill is so intrinsic to the everyday, normal tasks of young people—such as how to express affection—that steps to mastery are best designed by the adolescents themselves. In such a case adults may articulate a rationale regarding the need for the skill and then allow the adolescent(s) to develop a skill-building process in which adults provide counsel.

We can also help build skills for spiritual growth by giving adolescents a *vocabulary*. Acquiring a language related to one's relationship to God, the moral life, one's emotional experiences, and one's membership in the Church is a powerful aspect of skill-building. Adults can give young people the vocabulary to name sources of morality, the different kinds of relationships in life, signs of God's presence, components of their congregation's worship, the virtues that represent character and the vices that diminish it, the three dimensions of spiritual growth, components of the moral life, and so on. In short, building skills for spiritual growth includes intentionally giving youth a language with which they can name aspects of religious faith, moral living, and emotional awareness within the context of their specific denomination or religious tradition. Nevertheless, the process of building skills for spiritual growth is best served by a pedagogy that is language-light and experience-rich. Use fewer words and "go deeper sooner."

Teaching skills for spiritual growth requires the use of stories easily accessible by imagination and that mirror the stories lived by young people. It is also a pedagogy of reason, teaching adolescents to use rational thoughts in order to balance the impulsivity of emotions and the uncritical acceptance of certain cultural values. In addition, building skills for spiritual growth is an experience of faith that points to the love of God, the power of the Spirit, and the way of life exemplified by the central figure of one's faith: Christ for Christians, Muhammad for Muslims, Moses and the prophets for Jews, and so on.

Building skills for spiritual growth also involves the use of practice opportunities in which adolescents work on these skills as a way of life and faithful adults work on being an intrusive presence—always coaching, counseling, challenging, listening, clarifying, correcting, reinforcing, laughing, protecting, learning, and loving.

Building skills is often a case of incidental learning. We must recognize that skills often can be best taught in the quality of social interactions between the adult and the adolescent rather than between the student and the instructional material. Finally, building skills for spiritual growth involves a strong, fierce, and passionate sense of purpose—to introduce adolescents to skills for spiritual growth and authentic relationships that can help them successfully cope with the challenges of contemporary life and contribute to the common good within their communities of faith, friends, family, and citizens.

Those of you who seek to build skills for spiritual growth within a more structured educational setting might keep in mind the work done recently regarding multiple intelligences.[4] Some students have strengths in:

- Verbal-linguistic intelligence: They think in words and love reading and writing.
- Logical-mathematical intelligence: They think by reasoning and love exploring, calculating, and questioning.
- Visual-spatial intelligence: They think in images and pictures and love drawing, video, and other visual forms.
- Bodily-kinesthetic intelligence: They think through their senses and love moving, feeling, and hands-on activities.
- Musical-rhythmic intelligence: They think via melodies and sounds and love singing and vibrational effects.
- Interpersonal intelligence: They think by checking out ideas with others and love group discussions and common projects.
- Intrapersonal intelligence: They think by going deep inside themselves and love time alone, journaling, and other introspective dynamics.
- Naturalist: They are sensitive to the natural world and see connections and patterns within the plant and animal kingdoms.

Religious educators and youth ministers should employ poetry, stories, videos, group work, individual reflections, rhythmic ways of remembering skills, catch phrases, short informative essays, Scripture, and self-assessments in an attempt to address effectively a variety of different learning styles. Because of this variety of "intelligences," some educational activities will appeal to different types of learners at different times.

Educators are learning more and more about adolescents' need to see as well as to hear what they are being taught. Charts, posters, and other visuals will help adolescents learn and apply skills. Symbols also have a powerful way of capturing meaning in a language-light fashion, particularly appreciated by young people with low language skills. According to Charles Shelton:

> *Symbols provide the adolescent with a chance for self-expression that moves beyond the intellectual sphere. . . . For many adolescents, focusing on symbols can serve as a format within which ongoing questioning can take place . . . the use of symbols can enlarge the meaning and perspective that the person gives to his or her life.*[5]

Building skills for spiritual growth is not a precise activity. Regardless of the piloting, testing, measuring, and creative adaptations, building skills for spiritual growth is first and always a mystery. God's grace and our responses cannot be programmed but only experienced. Spiritual growth depends in part on the intrinsic motivation within each young person for adolescent motivation influences the building of skills. The mystery lies in the quality of the relationship between a young person's internal motivation and her or his transcendent God.

The Myth of Self-Esteem

Building skills for spiritual growth gives young people a sense of accomplishment, confidence in their ability to cope, and a strong sense of hope.[6] Most attempts at self-esteem building rest on this assumption: If youth feel good (about themselves), they will do well. Unfortunately, these kinds of approaches, which reinforce and remind young people of their innate self-worth, are based on a myth. William Damon, in his book *Greater Expectations,* includes this myth among the "misconceptions of modern times":

> *The notion that self-esteem is a prior cause of these positive outcomes derives, illegitimately, from correlational studies that*

show no more than simple association between measures of self-esteem and measures of achievement, health, and so on. Every statistics lesson taught anywhere begins by explaining that correlations do not establish causality. . . . In and of itself, self-esteem offers nothing more than a mirage for those who work with children. Like all mirages, it is both appealing and perilously deceptive, luring us away from more rewarding developmental objectives. While capturing the imagination of parents and educators in recent years, the mission of bolstering children's self-esteem has obscured the more promising and productive possibilities of child rearing. We would do better to help children acquire the skills, values, and virtues on which a positive sense of self is built.[7]

When researchers Elisabeth Hurd, Carolyn Moore, and Randy Rogers studied the parenting strengths of African-American families, they identified five common themes among effective parents: connection with family members, emphasis on achievement and effort, recognition of the importance of respect for others, cultivation of spirituality, and the ability to foster self-reliance.[8] Note that there is no mention of any self-esteem building efforts per se.

The truth is this, and the research data continue to reinforce it:

1. Adolescents in the United States already have very high self-esteem, even those young people who are incarcerated, addicted, pregnant, or withdrawn.

2. High self-esteem has not been proven to cause anything. Self-esteem correlates with several things, but researchers have, for the most part, found no causation with high self-esteem.[9]

3. In attempting to boost self-esteem, adults lower the hoops (expectations).[10] Academic hoops are lowered in this country's classrooms. Domestic hoops are lowered in this nation's living rooms. Moral hoops are lowered in this nation's culture. Hoops are lowered because of the mistaken assumption that young people will not attain the standards we set. We lower hoops because we think that failure will cause young people to feel bad about themselves and, as a result, not do well in general.

When *USA Weekend* conducted its eleventh annual teen survey in 1998, it asked 272,400 sixth- through twelfth-graders this question: "In general, how do you feel about yourself?" Forty-nine percent answered "really good," 44 percent answered "kind of good," 6 percent answered "not very good," and 1 percent answered "bad." Out of 272,400 young people, only 7 percent reported feeling "not very good" or "bad" about themselves.

On the other hand, when the same young people were asked, "Do you ever feel really depressed?" 16 percent answered "yes, often," 55 percent answered "occasionally," and 29 percent answered "no, never." In other words, although 93 percent of the 272,400 young people reported feeling "really" or "kind of" good about themselves, 71 percent of them reported being depressed "often" or "occasionally."[11]

This data illustrates the "mirage" of self-esteem. Adolescents do indeed experience depression, and the adults in their world notice it. However, it is not because of a lack of self-esteem, as caring adults conclude. Self-esteem is high. The cause of adolescent depression lies elsewhere. Perhaps it lies in a lack of hope. Perhaps it lies in broken dreams. Perhaps the adolescent experience of depression can be traced to matters of the spirit. Instead of assuming that if youth feel good about themselves, they will do well, the activity of building skills for spiritual growth assumes the reverse regarding self-esteem: *If youth do well, they will feel good about themselves.*

It is worth noting, however, that some adolescents do quite well and still feel depressed or lonely. Moreover, from a theological standpoint, it is important to remember that one does not earn God's unconditional love or favor. Nevertheless, the assumption that *when young people do well, they will feel good about themselves* holds greater potential than the traditional assumption when it comes to serving young people.

FOR REFLECTION

1. Imagine your efforts at facilitating adolescent spiritual growth as a pie cut into four slices: knowledge, attitudes, behaviors, and skills. Which slice is the biggest? In other words, to which of the four elements do you give the most attention or find yourself addressing first?

2. Which of the skills for spiritual growth listed in this chapter capture your interest the most?

3. Which skills do you think would be most helpful to the adolescent(s) for whom you care?

4. Which skills do you want to develop within your own spirituality?

5. What are your thoughts regarding self-esteem?

6. If you took a serious step away from assuming that *when young people feel good about themselves, they do well* and took a serious step toward the assumption that *when young people do well, they will feel good about themselves,* would the way you work with adolescents change? Why or why not?

7. Based on the sacred writings of your religion, what would God want you to teach adolescents about what it means to do well?

PRACTICALLY SPEAKING

- Building skills can be done informally within the normal flow of the day. You can reinforce skills while driving adolescents to an activity, working in the kitchen, or while watching television. It is not necessary to stop and "make a big production over it."
- Overcome any feelings of hesitancy that you may have. Despite the instructional and concrete nature of building skills, you will be pleasantly surprised at how open the adolescent is to brief and casual skill-building for spiritual growth.
- Be specific in the praise you give when you see a young person demonstrating a skill—or even partial components of a skill—for spiritual growth. It is not enough to say, "Good job." It is much more meaningful to describe exactly what the young person did well. You might say, "You don't think you have skills? I noticed

how you anticipated the way Mike might feel if you and your friends went to the movies without at least calling him and letting him know when and where he could meet you" or "Hey! You just mentioned the same Bible story that we heard last Sunday at church. Now you are applying it to this situation. You've got skills!!!"

Chapter 4

Honoring the Senses

A young person once told me the following:

"I'm in the marching band at school. We practice twice a day, before school and afterward. We practice all week long, and then we perform Friday night at halftime of the football game. When we finish our routine perfectly and start marching off the field to the cadence of the drummers, I look up in the stands and see people clapping, feel the music, and am full of pride. I feel so close to God right then. I'm smiling inside and almost want to cry at the same time, and I'm not sure why. But at that moment, I am so close to God."

Honoring the senses involves paying attention to, and staying focused on, the way young people talk about their experiences and is independent of any attempt to look for a truth learned or a virtue practiced.

Attending to stories, for the most part, is a *cognitive* function involving a young person's ability to think through a story, thereby recognizing truths and building on experience. Building skills, on the other hand, clearly represents a *behavioral* function in which a young person must learn *how* to do something concrete in improving one's religious faith, moral living, and/or emotional awareness. Honoring the senses calls us to consider this question: *In what ways can interested adults respond to the **affective** dimension of spiritual growth in adolescents?*

Honoring the senses is an activity that suggests that spiritual growth does not always involve a truth or a religious doctrine gleaned from sacred stories nor a behavior learned by building skills. It refers to the activity of paying attention to adolescent *emotionality* and *imagination*.

Emotionality: Rediscovering the Role of Emotions

If our efforts at fostering spiritual growth among adolescents remain focused exclusively on assimilating religious information, respecting certain moral values, and employing certain practices, we may be missing our opportunity to help young people open a very real door to the sacred.

In *Emile,* written by Jean Jacques Rousseau in 1758, the author spoke against teaching to the cognitive, rational dimension of students in facilitating spiritual growth:

It is one of the faults of our age to rely too much on cold reason, as if men were all mind. . . . In our attempt to appeal to reason only, we have reduced our precepts to words; we have not embodied them in deed. Mere reason is not active; occasionally she restrains, more rarely she stimulates, but she never does any great thing. Small minds have a mania for reasoning. Strong souls speak a very different language, and it is by this language that men are persuaded and driven to action.[1]

In the twentieth century Jacques Maritain gave priority to the affective or emotional dimension of human growth. In *Education at the Crossroads,* he wrote:

For a man and human life there is indeed nothing greater than intuition and love. Not every love is right, nor every intuition well directed or conceptualized, yet if either intuition nor love exists in any hidden corner, life, and flame of life are there, and a bit of heaven in a promise. Yet neither intuition nor love is a matter of training and learning; they are gift and freedom. In spite of all that, education should primarily be concerned with them.[2]

Nevertheless, formal attempts to influence the moral development of children and youth moved away from paying attention to emotions in the late 1960s. Jean Piaget built upon the analysis of Immanuel Kant by describing specific stages of development in which one's cognitive growth influenced one's moral development. Erik Erikson delineated eight psychosocial stages of development. Lawrence Kohlberg developed a theory of moral development that consisted of three levels and six stages of human growth.

More recent developmentalists have connected moral development to religious development. John Westerhoff in *Will Our Children Have Faith?* outlined four styles of faith that individuals embrace as they grow older. Westerhoff linked these styles of faith to chronological age, much like the psychosocial models of Piaget, Erikson, and Kohlberg.[3] In 1981 James Fowler, in his *Stages of Faith,* clearly included Piaget's and Kohlberg's stages and built upon them by outlining seven distinct stages covering one's life span.[4]

These cognitive-developmentalist views share the belief that as one grows in one's *reasoning ability,* one can grow into a deeper appreciation, understanding, and practice of the moral or religious life.

Such theories have given emotions a secondary, and extremely minimalistic, role to play in the moral and religious life. Consequently, a growing number of theorists have been raising voices of concern. In Charles Shelton's opinion:

> *Kohlberg is unable to maintain even an uneasy truce between cognition and affect. In essence, Kohlberg's position endorses the primacy of cognition. Relegating emotion to a secondary status in moral development, however, is clearly at variance with the historical traditions of many ethical and religious approaches to morality that note that emotion exercises a critical role in human moral experience.[5]*

Writing on morality, reason, and emotion in *Lawrence Kohlberg: Consensus and Controversy,* John Martin Rich observes the following:

> *Lawrence Kohlberg's cognitive moral development theory, while recognizing the emotions and other affective factors, does not provide a significant place for them. . . . The chief problem to Kohlberg's approach to emotions, however, is to assume that emotions are irrational or nonrational forces in conflict with the cognitive core of moral development rather than developing a cognitive view of emotions in relation to moral judgement.[6]*

Jerome Kagan in *The Nature of the Child* concluded that

> *Construction of a persuasive rational basis for behaving morally has been the problem on which most moral philosophers have stubbed their toes. I believe they will continue to do so until they recognize what Chinese philosophers have appreciated for a long time: namely, feeling, not logic, sustains the superego.[7]*

There is science behind emotionality. From a neurological perspective, the brain processes emotions as visual signals that go from the retina to the thalamus. There the message is translated for the brain and moves to the visual cortex, where it is analyzed for a response. If the response is emotional, it goes to the amygdala, which activates the emotional centers. However, a smaller signal often bypasses the visual cortex and goes straight to the amygdala in a quicker but less precise transmission. Therefore the amygdala can activate an emotional response before the rest of the brain can fully process all the information. Thus the key to emotional awareness may be one's ability to process more information before reacting to an immediate emotional response.

Researchers, in studying the emotional ability of young children, conclude that toddlers express and recognize emotion at an early age; they express "happy" at twenty months, "sad," "mad," and "scared" at thirty-six months, and recognize the emotions of others beginning around two and one-half years.[8] The task of managing emotions, now widely referred to as *emotional intelligence,* is a term first coined by Yale psychologist Peter Salovey and John Mayer of the University of New Hampshire in 1990.[9] Daniel Goleman, in *Emotional Intelligence,* explains that Salovey and Mayer's basic definition of emotional intelligence involves ability in these five domains:

1. "Knowing one's emotions," that is, the ability to recognize a feeling as it happens. This is the keystone of emotional intelligence. An inability to do so leaves one at the mercy of one's emotions.

2. "Managing emotions," that is, the ability to handle emotions in an appropriate way. This builds on the previous ability of identifying the emotion.

3. "Motivating oneself," that is, marshalling emotions in the service of a goal—be it achievement, bereavement, or redirection—for the purpose of a certain kind of productivity.

4. "Recognizing emotions in others," that is, the ability to be empathetic. This is a classical "people" skill with which one can pick up the subtle signals that indicate the needs and emotions of others. Inability in this area leaves one "emotionally tone deaf" and makes it difficult for one to help others.

5. "Handling relationships," that is, the ability to work with the emotions in others. This type of emotional intelligence enhances working relationships and results in authentic relationships and experiences of intimacy.[10]

The key premise to the notion of emotional intelligence as defined by Salovey, Mayer, and Goleman is that we can increase our level of emotional intelligence by intentionally developing certain practices. This is unlike the present understanding of IQ, which is seen as the amount of intelligence we are born with but that we cannot improve. Goleman's research has revealed that educators, counselors, and youth workers can indeed help young people increase their emotional intelligence with programs that have significant and measurable effects. Some programs have resulted in a decrease of fighting and aggression, teen pregnancies, and absenteeism, while increasing academic achievement, student satisfaction, and physical health.[11]

One of the more intriguing emotional intelligence efforts has been the Penn Depression Prevention Project directed by Martin Seligman, Karen Reivich, Lisa Jaycox, and Jane Gillham of the University of Pennsylvania. Their work, as described fully in their book *The Optimistic Child,* actually has been proven to help students learn how to intentionally decrease pessimism and increase optimism. The results include a measurable impact on self-reliance, school performance, resiliency, and physical health.[12]

While I am obviously encouraging the inclusion of emotionality in our understanding of spiritual growth, all of us should also ask:

> To what degree do the specifics of emotional intelligence reflect the values and characteristics held only by the economically successful, college-bound, white upper class?

> Who, or what, leads us to accept each of the specifics defining emotional intelligence?

> To what extent would the specifics of emotional intelligence be changed or enhanced if developed by a more integrated demographic, ethnic, and multicultural group?

J. A. Russell, in writing on "Culture, Scripts, and Children's Understanding of Emotion," points out that "people react emotionally to different things in different cultures" and adds that different cultures have different rules for displaying emotions. "These 'display rules' might dictate that at a funeral, for example, grief should be inhibited, displayed, or exaggerated."[13]

However, it is clear that theories such as emotional intelligence and the research conducted in this area restore the rightful place of emotions in considering the challenges, influences, and potential of adolescents' moral and religious journeys. The research relating to aspects of emotional intelligence can, and should, offset our reliance on cognitive development as the big key for moral and religious growth.

Emotions and Adolescent Spiritual Growth

And so we see that while the past cognitive-developmental views of moral growth (as your mind and reasoning ability grow, so does your level of moral reasoning) have made a contribution to our discussion around the moral life, such views have tended to neglect the human experience of emotions and their influence on the development of an adolescent's moral and religious life. In the past adults interested in participating in the spiritual journey of adolescents have not been encouraged by theorists, educators, and formal training to balance emphasis on cognitive development with respect for, and understanding of, the emotional dimension of adolescent spirituality. Why is this crucial?

First a word on why honoring emotionality is not crucial. I do not promote a distinct honoring of emotionality for the reasons given by others who have championed the cause of emotional intelligence. Such reasons include success in business, competence in social settings, academic achievement, or even physical health. Nor am I proposing that we honor emotionality because some proponents of emotional intelligence claim that it will increase sales for insurance salespersons, enable children to avoid depression, help adults handle the waxy build-up on the kitchen floor, come to terms with expanding waistlines, or control their anger when the children have misplaced the remote control to the television.

However, honoring emotionality among youth is crucial because adolescents may be the most emotional members of society. If we don't recognize that their emotions hold keys to their spiritual life, then we will be unable to accompany them on their journey of spiritual growth.

Will a teenager who is filled with rage have his or her moral life influenced more by emotions or by his or her cognitive stage of development? When a teenager experiencing a profound sense of loss, abandonment, or fear is faced with moral choices or religious opportunities, will she or he be more influenced by emotions or by her or his cognitive level? And what about love? Will that emotion have a primary or secondary influence on the moral and religious life of young people?

The activity of honoring the senses encourages interested adults to take seriously, or to honor, the emotional dimension of the adolescent's moral and religious life. This may be done by teaching young people to practice emotional awareness, inviting them to share their emotions, and helping young people recognize the deeper moral and religious truths found at the root of the emotions they experience in various situations. Underneath adolescent emotions lie the beliefs, ideals, principles, and dreams held most sacred by young people.

Norma Haan sees emotion as vital to our understanding of the moral life and reflects Rousseau's and Maritain's positions on the power of the affective:

> *Emotions accompany and enrich our understandings, and they convey far more authentic information about a person's position in a dispute than any well-articulated thoughts. In ordinary circumstances, emotions instruct and energize action. In situations of great moral costs, emotions can overwhelm and disorganize cognitive evaluations.[14]*

We should engage in the activity of honoring the senses because in doing so:

1. We help adolescents avoid becoming victims of their emotions and increase their ability to live the kind of moral and religious life their hearts deeply treasure. When interested adults honor emotionality in an adolescent, they can enable that young person to discover the deeper moral principle, religious belief, or soulful dream that evokes the emotion involved in a particular situation. When adults help young people discover the root of their emotions, they help them discover and understand what is sacred: truth, love, loyalty, authenticity, respect, fairness, integrity, virtue, peace, and compassion.

Shelton, in summing up his own convictions regarding the rightful place of emotions in the moral life, writes as follows:

> *In other words, we need to scrutinize the "ends" to which our emotions are directed . . . one place to begin this scrutiny is,*

again, to reflect on our desires. What, indeed, are our deepest desires? What do we value the most? Why do we say this? What do our desires say about ourselves as moral persons?[15]

2. We help adolescents recognize the emotions being experienced by others and, in doing so, develop crucial tools for moral living: empathy, compassion, and contribution to the common good.

3. We help young people reduce impulsivity and the dangerous impact it can have on them today, given the nature of contemporary culture.

Imagination

If truth is the daughter of time . . . then imagination must be the midwife presiding at the delivery.

M. Katherine Tillman[16]

Spiritual growth has a mystical side that is *felt, sensed,* and *imagined.* Young people literally sense God's presence in a hundred different ways: a joyous moment with a group of friends, a solitary moment in their bed at night, a kiss of nature's beauty, the sight of a newborn, love or affection from a friend or relative, and so on.

By honoring the imagination of adolescents, specifically the moral and religious imagination, interested adults will not only glimpse the spirituality of the young but also will foster its growth.

Maria Harris asks interested adults to enhance the work of developmentalists by considering art as a window to the sacred as well as the affective influence it has on moral growth.[17] Sharon Parks (1986) affirms the work of developmentalists such as Piaget, Kant, and Fowler and adds that when we integrate the past theories of development "with a robust understanding of imagination, the study of faith development may be seen as a study of the activity of Spirit."[18]

The Role of Imagination

The leaders of most of the world's religions spoke the language of religious imagination and with great success, because humans have the eyes to see and ears to hear mystery and the sacred, both of which transcend concrete, cognitive, and rational attempts to teach and explain. William Chittick explains the high degree of reverence given to imagination in the Sufi and Islamic faiths. He cites the writings of Ibn al-'Arabi, who defined imagination as the "Breath of the All-Merciful" and the Cloud:

Nothing is vaster [than imagination], since in its very reality, it governs all things and non-things. It gives form to sheer nonexistence, to the impossible, to Necessity, and to possibility. . . . Hence it perceives knowledge in the form of milk, honey, wine, or a pearl; it sees Islam as a dome or pillar; it sees the Qur'an in the form of butter and honey; it sees a debt in the form of a fetter; it sees God in the form of a human being or a light.[19]

In fact Chittick reminds us that imagination has been considered by Muslims to be one of the Five Divine Presences of God.[20]

The sacred sagas of the Old Testament (Hebrew Scriptures) depend on the use of religious imagination to communicate the experience of God: Eve's being tempted by the Devil in the form of a serpent to disobey God by eating a certain fruit; Cain's being permanently marked by God so that all humans would know of Cain's sin; Moses' talking to God in the form of a burning bush; Samuel's hearing God's voice in the wind; Jacob's wrestling with an angel of God who gives him a new name; God's flooding the earth for forty days; Lot's wife turning to a pillar of salt because of her disobedience; Joseph's interpretations of various dreams; Jonah in the belly of a whale, and so on.

Ryken writes of the biblical place of imagination:

The Bible repeatedly appeals to the intelligence through the imagination. . . . The one thing that it is not what we so often picture it as being: a theological outline with proof texts attached. When asked to define "neighbor," Jesus told a story. He constantly spoke in images and metaphors: "I am the light of the world," "You are the salt of the earth." . . . The point is not simply that the Bible allows for imagination as a form of communication. It is rather that the biblical writers and Jesus found it impossible to communicate the truth of God without using the resources of the imagination. . . . This all suggests that the imagination is a means by which God can reveal His truth and beauty and people can respond with due appreciation.[21]

Osage-Cherokee writer, teacher, and minister, Dr. George Tinker illustrates another role of religious and moral imagination, namely, its ability to shape the image people have of themselves as an individual and as a community:

> *Each individual recognizes herself or himself as a combination of qualities that reflect both sky and earth, spirit and matter, peace and war, male and female, and we struggle individually and communally to hold those qualities in balance with each other.*
>
> *. . . all creation is related and no one creature, human or otherwise, stands over or above another. The two lines forming a cross within the wagon wheel style circle symbolize the four directions of the earth, the four manifestations of Wakonta, the four cardinal virtues of a tribe, the four sacred colors of ceremonial life, the sacred powers of four animal nations, and the four nations of the two-legged (humans) that walk the earth (Black, Red, Yellow, and White).[22]*

Similarly, the founder of the Jesuit order of priests and brothers, Ignatius Loyola, promoted the application of senses as a way to enter more deeply into the mystery of Christ's life. His followers were taught a method of prayer involving the five senses of sight, smell, hearing, taste, and touch.[23]

As a lifelong professional in the field of youth work, I was oblivious to the role of the imagination. When I reviewed the literature regarding the impact of imagination on spirituality, I was astounded and embarrassed to discover an extraordinary amount of thought and theory surrounding the topic over the last three hundred years.

Modern writers, educators, and theologians are calling for a strong acceptance of the powerful role moral and religious imagination plays in providing humans with insight. Maria Harris's book, *Teaching and Religious Imagination,* represents a comprehensive treatment of the topic and its implications for work with young people. Harris observes:

> *The last several years have witnessed a remarkable burgeoning of interest in imagination, especially as it is related to the fields of philosophy, education, art, theology, and religious study. Works such as David Tracy's* The Analogical Imagination, *Elliot Eisner's* The Educational Imagination, *Lyn Ross Bryant's* Imagination

and the Life of the Spirit, *John Dixon's* Art and Theological Imagination, *and Walter Brueggemann's* The Prophetic Imagination *are symptomatic of this interest. From one perspective, I am convinced that such interest expresses what W. H. Auden once spoke of as a 'wild prayer of longing' resting at the core of the human spirit.*[24]

Most of the views published on imagination are both complex and contradictory. Imagination was nearly dismissed during the rationalist era of the Enlightenment because it was considered to be closely associated with fantasy, feelings, and art. However, the views expressed over the last three hundred years by Keats, Blake, Wordsworth, Kant, Coleridge, Ricoeur, Kierkegaard, Corbin, Eliade, and many others enhanced the understanding and appreciation of imagination for its ability to help humans make meaning, conceptualize the sacred, articulate mystery, envision the better state of the common good, and respect the human potential.[25]

Immanuel Kant's view is considered the first and strongest step away from the Enlightenment's minimalistic interpretation of imagination and toward a highly respectable appreciation of imagination. Kant viewed imagination as *einbildungskraft*—the human power to make logical understandings of the matter found in life and creation.[26]

In 1797 Samuel Taylor Coleridge built upon Kant's vocabulary of imagination by offering us a distinction between primary and secondary imagination. According to Coleridge, primary imagination is used in our everyday tasks of fusing together various sensations with reasonable explanations, understandings, and expressions. Secondary imagination, on the other hand, breaks down human thoughts and experiences and re-creates them in art, poetry, sculpture, and so on. In this sense, primary imagination is the everyday functional dimension of imagination, while secondary imagination is the creative and expressionistic dimension of imagination.[27]

Soren Kierkegaard cautioned against an uncritical infatuation with imagination, but he nevertheless placed imagination at the center of the moral and religious life. He maintained that imagination helped a person do two things: imagine what one can become and imagine the good one can do. This placed imagination at the core of human power.[28]

This interplay of imagination and will, particularly between *moral imagination* and will, provides the foundational reason that caring adults can facilitate adolescent spirituality by honoring adolescent imagination.

Oftentimes young people can imagine the right thing to do but may lack the will to make the hard choices, the strength to postpone immediate need gratification, practice perspective taking, and so on. Paying attention to the moral and religious imagination of the young and helping them see, feel, and exercise their religious and moral imagination [20] opens a doorway to spirituality for both the interested adult and the adolescent.

Moral imagination can have a greater influence on adolescents than moral intelligence. John Henry Newman maintained that the working together of imagination and reasoning results in solid moral conscience and religious faith.

Harris offers four kinds of religious imagination: contemplative, ascetic, creative, and sacramental.

Contemplative imagination incorporates the active intensity of attending, listening, being with, and existing fully in the presence of Being. It incorporates the cleanness of mind and clarity of sight that enables awareness of the other. It is a reminder of the mystical possibilities which reside within us all.

Ascetic imagination is a kind of distancing which brings to bear all the understandings associated with religious discipline and discipleship. These include the need for detachment in the presence of the other, the letting be of being, the standing back in order not to violate. . . . The ascetic imagination helps the teacher teach sympathetically and empathetically, but always with reverence and respect other people demand and need. The ascetic imagination can act as a guarantor of the sacred in every human being.

Creative imagination enables us to see that the status quo can always be changed. What seem like final solutions are seen to be merely tentative. Creative imagination allows us to tap into our potential in the service of one another and the world.

Sacramental imagination empowers us to see the revelation of mystery, "as well as the presence of the holy, the gracious, and the divine" in all of life and in all of human work.[29]

Such an honoring, or understanding, of imagination serves us well in our work with young people. Helping adolescents exercise their contemplative imagination enables them to slow down in the midst of their frenetic pace in order to get in touch with their God. Helping adolescents exercise their ascetic imagination enables them to detach from emotionally charged situations, avoid impulsive reactions, and respect the dignity of others who may be different or difficult. Helping adolescents exercise their creative imagination enables them to improve their potential to solve problems, reach goals, and keep dreams alive. Helping adolescents exercise their sacramental imagination makes it easier for them to recognize God in ordinary and extraordinary exchanges, events, music, accomplishments, failures, losses, rituals, and traditions.

Adolescents use their imagination to make meaning of their lives and, ultimately, of their spirituality. Sharon Daloz Parks writes:

> *For the composing of meaning as the most comprehensive—most ultimate and intimate—dimension of consciousness, we reserve the word "faith." Meaning and faith are composed by means of the imagination. . . . It is by means of images, metaphors, and symbols that we shape into one the chaos of our existence, that we simplify and unify, that we apprehend, though we can never comprehend—the real. It is by means of the disciplined imagination that we search out fitting and right images by which to apprehend truth and compose the meanings we shall live by.[30]*

Sometimes it helps to have a sense of humor when honoring religious imagination. A friend of mine who is a Catholic priest once told me:

> *Every night my father would sit before the picture of the Sacred Heart [of Jesus], which he cut out of a calendar and framed. He felt that God must be very tired from listening to everyone's troubles, so father would sit in front of this picture of Jesus and tell God jokes he had heard that day. From my father, I learned the virtue of laughter. And laughter is a virtue!*

Another told me:

> *All my friend Josie talks about is the Virgin Mary's messages to her. How do you tell your friend to get a life? I mean, if the*

Virgin Mary's visiting our church, fine. I can accept that. But if Mary's coming to our church four times a day, seven days a week, then maybe SHE needs to get a life!

Honoring Imagination for Spiritual Growth

I asked some young people which symbol(s) in their religious traditions meant the most to them and why. One young man responded, "The symbol that means the most to me in my Church is the incense." I asked him why, thinking he would mention something about how the rising smoke symbolizes our prayers ascending to God's ear in heaven. Instead, he said, "The incense reminds me that you pray best after you get burned."

Imagination helps young people learn lessons not spoken and see truths not addressed. Interested adults can facilitate adolescent spirituality by honoring and learning from the language of the imagination as spoken by young people. We can honor adolescent imagination and the way youth use imagination to make meaning, by deliberately paying attention to—and asking questions about—the words adolescents use, the songs they love, the images they value, and the places that mean the most to them.

These are the elements that make up the language of moral and religious imagination among young people. They speak of the motivating dreams of adolescents. We can tap into the imagination behind the dreams of young people in order to help youth think critically.

Benedict Guevin, in writing about moral imagination, cites the work of Kathleen Fischer:

> *Imagination is the vehicle which conveys us out of our own world and into the world of others, from the state of being closed in on self to a state of openness, from unwillingness to change to prospects of a new horizon. The imagination, then, is the means by which persons allow the Christian vision, as it is encountered in those formative stories of Christian community, to shape the moral life.[31]*

Guevin also quotes Stanley Hauerwas: "What is lacking is not a better moral calculus of what acts Christians should and should not do, but an enlivening of the imagination by images that do justice to the central symbol of our faith."[32]

Why honor imagination? It becomes clear that imagination is the tool by which adolescents can envision the kind of peace promoted by most of the world's major religions. It is the means by which adolescents can navigate their moral life, sense the sacred, and experience the mystery and love of God.

Imagination is the tool that helps adolescents recognize God in others, maintain authentic and caring relationships, and hear the call to service. It is also clear that imagination has a language of metaphors expressed in religious and secular symbols among young people and which may or may not be understood or appreciated by the adult culture or even a different subculture of young people themselves.

David Loomis reminds us that the volumes written on imagination by philosophers, scientists, mystics, and managers throughout history tell us that "Imagination is the cognitive faculty that mediates a person's relationship to God."[33] Referring to Scripture, Loomis writes:

> *So crucial is imagination for entering and perceiving God's realm of pure possibility that Scripture, with few exceptions, addresses us imaginatively. . . . Imagination operates through every sensory modality (auditory, visual, olfactory, tactile, gustatory, and kinesthetic), as well as beyond them in acts of linguistic and mathematical creativity.[34]*

Loomis's recent research on the importance of imagination on faith formation refers to a dimension of imagination that leads to insight. It is precisely this *insightful* dimension of imagination that enables adolescents to recognize truth, beauty, and love as signs of God's presence. Moreover, it enables adolescents to deepen their understanding of themselves as children of God, related to all others in the family of God.

The research of David Loomis shows a high correlation between *imagination for insight* and a mature level of spiritual awareness involving appreciation for theological paradox and mystery, openness to the insights and values of other traditions, and mastery of one's own religious tradition.

He recommends that interested adults foster a growth of imagination for insight in several ways: by providing opportunities for young people to play; by providing them with opportunities for introversion in which they can be still enough to contemplate and visualize matters of the spirit; by providing opportunities for creative expression; and by engaging them in storytelling.[35]

Similarly, Brenda Lealman's study of 6,576 adolescents in the United Kingdom on the relationship between young people, spirituality, and imagination affirms and challenges the current approaches of those interested in teaching for spiritual growth:

> *Our findings suggest that young people are able to recognize in their experience what is religiously significant. This indicates a capacity to use unlearned, intuitive forms of knowledge. But the research shows that existing forms of education do little to assist the individual to synthesize learned and unlearned forms of knowledge. Where this is happening most clearly seems to be where the imagination is activated to work creatively on the paradoxes that emerge from tension between these ways of knowing.[36]*

Along the same lines, Ryken concludes:

> *To sum up, all people, including Christians, need the truth and beauty that imagination can impart. That truth and beauty are needed during the week, and on Sunday. The nature of truth is such that it can never be adequately expressed or experienced only as an abstraction or as a set of facts. Truth also requires the story, the poem, the paint on canvas, the sound of music.[37]*

Such an understanding and an honoring of the language of religious and moral imagination can help us hear adolescent music on a deeper level. Max Stackhouse maintains that the role of the bard throughout the ages has been to give expression to moral and religious imagination through song and theater:

> *What gives this music depth is this: the music of the bard was not only its artistry, but its capacity to frame the moral and spiritual meanings . . . in a way that is distinct from its closest civilizational relative—the law. . . . What the law establishes from the outside in, the arts establish from the inside out. The bard, the musician, and the poet are thus the necessary allies of religious and cultural values.[38]*

Stackhouse maintains that when today's music addresses issues related to spirituality, especially to the ultimate meaning and end of life on Earth, then music can and does play a role in the development or reinforcement of religious imagination:

This dimension of life can only be captured by imaginative vision, by the kind of rapture that drives gifted people into composition, performance, and communication. They make it possible for others to hear and see and taste glimpses of that which is not and cannot yet be. . . . Such awareness touches us all. Every believer is something of an artist, and every artist lives on the brink of religious vision.[39]

This may also explain why religious art may have inspired more followers than any written teaching or dogma. Brett Webb-Mitchell writes that:

In order to give our imaginations a stage or empty canvas, and a means or tool for expression, human beings need some form of representation in order to share with others what they have imagined. These forms of representation are the pictures, speech, dance, hand gestures, words, numbers, computer graphics, and songs that become the devices that enable us to share our internal, private impressions.[40]

Mitchell's work with learning-disabled and behaviorally-impaired youth leads to the conclusion that applies to adults who wish to work with *any* adolescent:

The discovery and the understanding of our experience of God is facilitated by and through the imagination of our hearts and minds. We see the revealing power of the human imagination in a religious context and an activity even in the lives of children who have been labeled as having "behavioral disorders."[41]

Honoring religious imagination among adolescents challenges interested adults to seek the deeper truths expressed in the music, media, and symbols that seem so important to young people. The key to this way of honoring religious imagination and pointing out the deeper truths is that it must always be done with respect for the passionate convictions of young people. In one of his last public speeches in the United States, Paulo Freire addressed this point:

> *Revealing truth and highlighting beauty cannot be intolerant activities. To highlight beauty, for example, in an intolerant manner would in itself be an ugly act. It is an indignity to speak of truth which one is revealing without respect for the person who would reveal it differently. It is almost as bad as one who would hide the truth.*[42]

Research goes on to show that religious imagination is often in play as adolescents preserve memories[43] and cherish certain possessions. According to Hirschman and LaBarbera, people use imagination to "enshrine" some possessions as sacred. Specifically, they fall into the following categories:

1. Possessions that represent one's past and personal memories (i.e., that enshrined one's selfhood):

   "My piano—it represents all my dreams—past, present, and future."

   "A carved wooden doll—my father gave it to me when I was nine because it looked like me."

   "My photo album keeps memories alive, so I can relive the events."

   "A Pebbles Flintstone doll, given to me when I was two years old and in the hospital. My Uncle Izzy gave her to me, and she was my favorite. . . . I took Pebbles everywhere. . . . Her stuffing is coming out. . . . When I was four I washed her and cut her hair. She currently has a ponytail in the middle of her head but is bald all around it. . . . I'll never part with Pebbles. There are too many tears and memories between us.

2. Possessions that link the individual to relationships with loved ones, both living and deceased (i.e., that enshrined one's relationship to others; facilitated self-transcendence):

   "My grandmother's scarves and earrings. . . . I used to watch my grandmother's primping and knew that someday I would do those things, too. I would spend many hours at my grandmother's bureau playing with tangerine-colored lipsticks and fancy rouge,

pretending to be a grown-up lady. . . . When my grandmother died, all I asked for were the scarves and earrings, and I was so very happy when I was given them. . . . Others may perceive these scarves as cheap and frail; however, they will always be priceless to me because they hold the most precious memories in the world and represent a love that will never die."

3. Possessions that are specifically religious (i.e., that enshrined one's relationship to a deity). However, such religious "possessions" were not necessarily material objects, such as one's Bible. Also included among religious possessions were *relationships* with family, friends, and God.[44]

By using their imagination in sustaining memories, adolescents maintain their favorite images of self. David Elkind, in *All Grown Up and No Place to Go,* implies that such memories are strung together by adolescents to form the "personal fable" of self from which they make sense of their life's journey. Adolescents also develop an "imaginary audience" of significant peers and adults who, in the mind of the young person, notice everything and have certain expectations of him or her. Elkind advises interested adults to take seriously the adolescent use of imagination as they discover how young people operate out of their own "private logic" in decision making.[45]

Interested adults who honor the senses of adolescents will do well in taking the time to discover and reverence the "personal fables," "imaginary audiences," and "private logic" of the young people in their lives, without necessarily agreeing with or condoning the accuracy of such imaginations.

Finally, those of us participating in the spiritual growth of adolescents may find it helpful to understand the functions of imagination described by James Roy King in terms of different kinds of spiritual "moments." Imagination leads to:

1. "Aha" moments of discovery, enlightenment, and revelation of the sacred. Such moments have been described by Buddhists as *satori.*

2. "Moments of moral or religious confrontation," which are usually unexpected and intense.

3. "Moments that are historical or eventful" in that they mark something of moral or religious significance in one's life and spiritual journey. The great religious traditions of the world employ much imagination in understanding their historical moments: Moses parting the Red Sea; Abraham's willingness to sacrifice his son; Elijah defeating the prophets of Baal; Jesus' birth, death, and resurrection; Allah revealing the Qur'an to Muhammad; and so on.

4. "Moments of grace, in which one is blessed by an act of God" and experiences the providence of God by being strengthened, protected, or enriched. Such moments of grace can be experienced in unexplainable ways or through the wonderful charity of others.

5. "Moments related to place(s)" where one can count on experiencing some aspect of the sacred, usually related to truth, beauty, or love. Again, the world's religions cherish moments in such holy places. Muslims seek to visit Mecca and arrive with the great cry of *labbayaka*, meaning "I am here, Lord." Jews reverence visits to the Western Wall and during Passover proclaim, "Let us go to the house of the Lord." Christians value the Holy Land. Religious persons everywhere count on the daily, weekly, and seasonal encounters of the sacred in places of worship: churches, temples, mosques, and synagogues.[46]

Honoring the senses by respecting the different kind of "moments" in which adolescents use their God-given religious imagination, while at the same time remembering the great difficulty many adolescents have in expressing themselves, will increase your ability to understand the struggle of adolescents to name and describe their personal experiences of the Spirit.

For us, the challenge does not lie in a lack of spirituality among adolescents, but rather in a lack of opportunities for young people to unpack, explore, exercise, and express the real and authentic experience of God, which they sense through their imagination and emotions.

FOR REFLECTION

1. Rousseau wrote, "Mere reason is not active; occasionally she restrains, more rarely she stimulates, but she never does any great thing. . . . Strong souls speak a very different language, and it is by this language that men [and women] are persuaded and driven to action." When have you been driven to do a "great thing" with a "strong soul"? What emotions drove you? What language did your soul speak? What did you realize was sacred to you?

2. What emotions are most obvious in the adolescents for whom you care?

3. What do these emotions reveal about what that person (or group) holds as sacred?

4. How has emotionality influenced your spiritual growth?

5. What symbol within your religious tradition means the most to you and why?

6. How does humor contribute to your spirituality?

7. Name a possession that you hold to be "sacred." What does it say to you?

8. Think about an adolescent for whom you care. What do you imagine is his or her "personal fable"—the story that young person believes about himself or herself?

9. How do you think that a young person's "imaginary audience" influences the decisions he or she makes?

10. Imagine the moments that have impacted your spirituality. Were they moments of discovery, confrontation, significant events, blessing, or place?

11. How can you help the adolescents for whom you care to name their important spiritual moments?

PRACTICALLY SPEAKING

- Remember the fundamental way of honoring adolescent emotionality and imagination: *Be quiet and listen carefully.* Make mental notes to yourself as to what the young person's comments reveal about what his or her heart holds sacred.

- When and if you do speak, do not try to help the adolescent solve a problem. That, literally, is the *last thing* to do. You can (and should) offer to help with the problem at a later time. If you choose to speak, intentionally ask questions that will help the young person or persons *talk further and deeper* about their emotions and/or imagination. This is precisely what honoring the senses involves.

- Occasionally entertain and evoke imaginative and emotional comments with playful questions, such as:

"If God played hide-and-seek with you and was hiding from you for a long time, what place, activity, or person or group would you seek out because you believe that is where or how you will feel God's presence?"

"If you could talk to any biblical character, to whom would you want to talk? What would you ask that person? What might that person say to you in response?"

"Which one of your religion's symbols, holy days, or songs is your favorite?"

Chapter 5

Offering Solidarity

Susie, one of the local triplets in town, is placed in a drug rehabilitation center. Susie and her parents ask you to come and participate in her opening therapy session.

Peter is killed in a car accident. His friends are traumatized. One asks you how God could do such a thing.

Your nephew Jeff, a straight-A student and a wonderful kid, wants to talk to you during his parents' anniversary party. He says he's attracted to a friend of the same gender. He wants to know if you think it's all right to be gay.

Shannon, a leading member of your volleyball team, is rumored to be developing a serious drinking problem.

You discover that your oldest child, a high school senior, had sex in your house while you and your spouse were out of town.

While you are driving your daughter and three other sophomore girls to a high school dance, Ellen, the quiet one, asks you and the others in the car if you believe that suicide is a sin.

You and two of your friends are driving on the highway, returning from a conference in the middle of a snowstorm. You notice a teenager walking in the storm along the highway, miles between the last and next exit. You stop and pick him up. He says everything is fine and that he's just walking. When you ask him if he is running away, he nods yes.

Harvey, an eighteen-year-old from a broken home who is living on his own, calls you around midnight. He has just found out that Adele, his girlfriend of seven months, is pregnant. He has decided to get married next weekend and wants you to stand up for him at the wedding. You explain all your reservations and concerns. Nevertheless, he says, "I'm going to be a man and marry Adele. Will you please be in my wedding?"

Darren's uncle has decided to pull him off your basketball team because of failing grades. You support the decision and offer to help in *any way you can. Two days later the uncle calls to tell you that he is has given up: Darren has been placed on in-school suspension for fighting.*

All of the above situations are real. All represent some of the tougher, yet common, challenges that come to adults involved in the spiritual growth of young people.

What kind of effort and sensibilities are required of us?

Who wants to be involved in the spiritual growth of adolescents?

What should be the qualities and characteristics of our relationships with young people?

How should we handle situations like the ones just described?

Of the three spiritual growth activities we have looked at so far, one revolves around cognitive thinking (attending to stories), one focuses on behaviors (building skills), and one centers on the affective (honoring the senses).

Our fourth and final activity, *offering solidarity,* represents the relational dynamic of being present to young people in certain ways. Note well, however, that *offering* solidarity it is not the same as standing in solidarity, because sometimes young people don't want or need us to "stand up" for anything, but rather to sit down next to them.

Offering solidarity respects the fact that sometimes when we, as caring adults, join uninvited in solidarity with an individual or a group, we inadvertently rob that person or group of the opportunity to stand (or sit) alone. In doing so, we may rob that young person or group of dignity.

While directing the very first Teaching for Spiritual Growth Institute, I witnessed an incredible exchange that illustrates the ironies of standing in solidarity instead of offering it:

The discussion centered on helping those who are poor. One Caucasian woman described the event that turned her life around and propelled her into a twenty-year career as an exemplary teacher committed to teaching among those who are poor in the Bronx. She described how as a young adult she had been part of a group of young college students who would get on a bus one Saturday a month and go into the poorest inner city neighborhoods to help clean up city streets, renovate buildings, shovel snow in the winter, and help those who were poor in any way they could. She shared how these experiences opened her eyes to economic injustice and how the people she encountered seemed so strong and full of moral fiber. She went on to say exactly how these experiences fed her soul and fired her spirit to work for the common good. It was a genuine moment of authenticity on her part.

Yet when she finished, another woman, who was a principal from an elementary school in Washington, D.C., where her students ducked gunfire regularly, said, "You were on those buses?! I lived in that neighborhood as a little girl. And every time those yellow buses pulled into our neighborhood, I would go to my mother and ask, 'Mama, why do these white people come into our neighborhood with their brooms and stuff? Do they think we can't keep our own porches clean? Do they think we can't take care of ourselves, that there's something the matter with all of us?' And my mother would just shrug as if she had no idea why you felt that you had to come. I can see how this was a powerful experience for you. Can you see how it made those of us feel who lived there?"

So it is with this powerful activity of offering solidarity to youth: You must always be ready to accept their decline of your offer. Sometimes adolescents will not be able to verbalize their willingness to accept or decline an offer of solidarity, so you must learn to read their body language, the sparkle or dullness in their eyes, or honor the sense you get while in their midst. Yet when caring adults do stay in solidarity with young people, adolescents find those adults to be trusted friends who accompany them as they make amends, listen to their frustrations, advocate their well-being, sit with them in the bleachers, help them with a project, insist on shaking their hand with every greeting, regularly inquire about the condition of their lives, talk them out of making poor decisions, help them find jobs, and ask questions that matter.

Throughout this book, we have considered the thoughts and writings of theorists and researchers. For the purpose of illuminating the complexity, necessity, paradoxes, challenges, and truth involved in offering solidarity, I now offer the following collection of comments made by dedicated and exemplary professionals who relate to young people every day and who consistently deal with the kinds of situations presented at the beginning of this chapter. The following comments come from adults who have sustained a life of service to the spiritual growth of young people within a variety of settings and roles: teachers, youth ministers, coaches, administrators, and other youth-serving professionals. I recorded them during five sessions of the Teaching for Spiritual Growth Institute.

Their comments, in their own words, represent the wisdom gained from working directly with young people—often in very difficult situations—and speak to different dimensions of offering solidarity to young people.[1]

Areas of Solidarity

We can offer solidarity to young people in nine different areas:

Area 1: Moral Courage

"Schools have diminished moral inventories and elevated academic inventories. We have huge celebrations over test scores, but what celebrations are there for moral accomplishments?"

"We talk about racism in big terms: Latinos, Asians, sexism, and so on. But it's more intimate. It's about conversation: me and you. And the vocabulary we use should be sin and conversion."

"We now have a technology in which the perimeter elements of our culture, for example, pornography, violence, and so on, are now into the center of our 'common'—into the core of our imagination."

"Healthy bodies are great. Good education is great. Yogurt and yoga are great, and getting rid of stress is great . . . but FOR WHAT? FOR WHAT?"

"What are we willing to say is totally reprehensible? Over what will we express moral outrage with kids? When are we willing to say flat out something is flat-out sinful?"

"Fostering spiritual growth in kids includes keeping hope alive and a certain amount of moral outrage."

"We are called to be compassionate, but we are also called to be more than that. To be transforming we sometimes have to say, 'Sin no more.' Sometimes we can be tempted by compassion."

"I have found out that finding a tone for my moral voice and knowing the right volume level to share it with kids is a spiritual task. It calls me to discern the Spirit in the moment and, in a sense, learn how to be—or not to be—a theologian on my feet."

Area 2: Advocacy

"Rescue kids any way you can."

"If you drop a frog into boiling water, it will jump out and save itself. But if you put it in lukewarm water and very slowly turn up the heat . . . click . . . click . . . the frog will burn to death. Be very aware of when that kind of slow burning is happening to a young person."

"We live in a world where if you don't ask, 'Why are young people crying?' then who will? We are the ones closest to that question. Keep asking that question until we can hear another one: 'Why are young people laughing?' and 'Why are young people dreaming?' Being with teens without a function of advocacy is an ego trip by adults who want to relive their adolescence."

"I worry about three kinds of kids: 'visitors,' who are like tourists, just checking life out but not making any serious investment; 'victims,' who are getting ripped off by circumstances they have not caused; and 'vampires,' who are sucking the life out of other kids."

"I'm never in real solidarity with the kids I work with, but I do hear the same sirens, angry fights, dirt, heat, sleepless nights . . . and I share the same question with them: 'What are we going to do?'"

"When you care, you get the reciprocity of respect."

"We must always ask, 'Is there any little thing we can do?' I think there is. I think any small, good thing that we can do for kids on their journey will make a difference in their spirituality."

"I had worked so long with Clinten, and he had made such progress. But he lost control one day for one second. Then it immediately escalated, and administrators and other kids got involved. He had a learning disability. . . . He locked himself in the bathroom. The cops came like a Swat team . . . with guns. I talked Clinten out of the bathroom and into my office. I couldn't say anything to him. All I could do was handle this overwhelming rage inside of me regarding the way the situation was handled. I left the room to talk to an administrator. By the time I returned, the police had led him away in handcuffs. When I sat down, I noticed that Clinten had left me a note. It reflected our many conversations about a poster hung in my classroom, which became our motto. He wrote (misspelled): 'Hold fast to dreams.'"

Area 3: Achievement

"I am convinced that the most important thing that young people need is a positive sense of purpose. Ambition! Aspiration! Self-esteem is not built on empty affirmation but on a thousand small victories and skill-building challenges that are hard at first."

"I don't believe we need to tell kids how good they are but rather help them learn what they need to know in order to succeed."

"Write this down: When you hear excuses, you got to keep saying to kids, 'I don't care.'"

"Getting kids on teams—not just athletic teams, but well-coached units—has a transforming power to help them discover what they don't know that they didn't know."

"We can provide structure and strength to kids who come to us. They look for us to provide that. I was in sixth grade during the New York City blackout in 1963. I thought I could use this as an excuse for not doing my homework. The next day my teacher asked me for my homework. When I explained about the blackout, she said, 'Mr. Brown, didn't you have any candles?'"

"I always make sure that my kids keep their shoes shined. When they come back to me after going through college, they say to me, 'Hey, look—my shoes are still shined.'"

"Kids know that when they come near me, they will tuck in their shirts and pull up their pants. I don't care what other people let them do. When you are with me, you live with my rules."

"Spiritual growth today involves helping young people develop a concrete sense of tomorrow. We must convey a spirituality that believes that if we and they act a certain way today, it will affect what we have tomorrow."

Area 4: Religious Experience

"Assume that each young person has a deep hunger for God. Don't worry about it, and don't be surprised by it. Get below the below. Help them get to that awareness. Help them touch it."

"More often now, people want a religious moment, not a psychological one. Why don't we help them have one?"

"I would propose that the hunger for spiritual growth is not an option. It is by design; it is the copyright of being human. Our excesses—be they food, drink, drugs, sex, or work—are signs that we are attending to our natural spiritual hunger."

"People co-teach spiritual growth when they are teaching other things. Teaching for spiritual growth is not a separate subject matter. It happens when you are engaged in life. You, as a teacher of spiritual growth, must recognize spiritual growth as it goes down and do something with it. Spiritual teachers constantly ask, 'Is this grist for the mill'? The kid you are talking to is struggling with math; is it 'grist for the mill'? Another is having trouble with a coach; is it 'grist for the mill'? Someone is being mistreated; is it 'grist for the mill'? Can you get to some aspect of spiritual growth with any of these experiences of life? Is God giving you and the young person any spiritual insights with this 'material'?"

"Malcolm X's transformation didn't come from 'group therapy' or federal programs. He was saved by powerful religious experiences."

"A kid told me that he feels like everything rains down on him. But he told me that in church on Sunday, he feels like an umbrella is over him, keeping him out of the rain . . . and by next Saturday his umbrella is all weathered and worn."

"Spirituality includes a real degree of gratitude. Be grateful for the sweet, good things in life."

"Feed the hunger of adolescents. Touch the hostility. And invite them to imagine trusting and being worthy of trust."

Area 5: The Search for Truth

"You want to know why people are dying a spiritual or emotional death? It's because truth hasn't found a home."

"Truth is more contagious than deceit."

"Help them take a long, loving look at the real."

"Racism starts at an early age. Other teams won't come to play at our field unless we guarantee that we'll have eight police officers at a football game and two at a basketball game. Then our kids come, see all the cops, get the message, and laugh."

"A sixth-grade student slept in my classroom one night. Her face was all bruised by being stepped on and hit the night before. I found her in my room the next morning and called her mother, who said that the girl didn't want to go to the hospital, and she didn't think it was safe to stay home. The mother and daughter thought it was best for her to sleep in my classroom. It was the safest place they could think of. After I spent some time taking care of the girl and having her checked, I returned to my sixth-grade class. They had elected one youngster as a spokesman who said to me in one voice, 'Now do you know what we have been talking about? Now do you know what we are living with?' And then I realized that I was teaching too hard. I had really been preaching to those kids and I had no understanding of them. It took a class of twelve-year-olds to teach me how to be a better teacher. From that moment on, I changed the way I taught."

Area 6: Spiritual Direction

"The kids I work with have an innate sense of spirituality, but they lack hope. The purpose of those of us who work with youth is one that leads them out of—and at the same time, more inside of—themselves."

"*Where* you talk from determines what you will get back from young people. Talk from your mind of ideas, and you will get into mind fights. But talk from your spirit or your soul, and you will get a response of the spirit."

"Spiritual direction is affectionate direction."

Area 7: School-Related Issues

"I was called into my firstborn's kindergarten class, and they told me he was developmentally disabled. As a parent, not as an educator, I took him out of that school and had him tested at Columbia University. They found that he had a learning disability. They couldn't quite test him. He had trouble decoding words and writing, but they insisted that he was very bright. . . . He turned out to be a cellist. . . . Last night he played at the White House."

"The parents told me that the school had told them to put their son on Ritalin. They did not do so but told the school that they had. After a while the teacher started writing notes home to the parents telling them how well their son was doing. One note read 'Your son has earned sixteen bonus points this quarter and things have really changed now that he's on his medication.'"

"My daughter was trying to apply to Cornell, but because she is a minority, the counselor told her not to. He told her, 'They won't accept you.' I told her to aim high, and she got accepted. The counselor then told her, 'That's nice, but it's very, very difficult. Do you really think you can stay with it for four years?' Well, my daughter graduated from Cornell. Then she went on and got her master's degree from MIT. Now she is working on her Ph.D. at MIT."

"What's the deal? I spend more time worrying about the kid balancing the pencil on his nose while ignoring the kid who makes straight A's and looks down on, and snickers at, the kid who makes C's."

Area 8: Pain

"In our neighborhood, a sign of respect is that your house does not get tagged [spray-painted] with graffiti by the gangs. Well, I went to the house of one of my Asian students, and her house was completely tagged with graffiti."

"There is always the tendency to focus on correcting the aggressor when one kid does wrong to another. But I insist on focusing on the victim and noticing that person's pain. I help that kid express his or her pain, embarrassment, or frustration. Then I make sure that the aggressor becomes aware of the pain caused."

"Sometimes it is not a question of raising hell, but rather it is a question of lowering a little bit of heaven for young people."

"Be with the pain, not the physical pain, but the spiritual pain that comes with broken dreams. And it's a spiritual thing to handle the pain of broken dreams."

"We have to attend to their pain, but we also must teach them to move past their pain. I have to keep telling kids that life is more than their experience of pain. Good-byes are followed by new hellos."

Area 9: Passions

"Every passion is a clue to our desire for God. Can we engage young people to talk about their passions?"

"I am married to a Mexican, and we adopted a boy from Mexico when he was four days old. He is very dark, and we live in a white neighborhood. I thought all I had to do was love him, but it's more complicated than that. On the first day of kindergarten, the other boys made fun of him, told him to go home and take a bath so his color would lighten up. Once, while watching TV, he jumped up and yelled at the TV, 'I wish I had parents with skin like me!' Eventually he befriended a neighborhood boy who is Japanese and was adopted by Caucasian parents like us. I used to listen outside my window as they told each other stories of the names they had been called that week in school. . . . Recently, Bill Moyers came to town. My son shared the stage with him because today my son is an accomplished poet."

Adult Attributes

The activity of offering solidarity is effective when we can demonstrate any of the following attributes.

A. Personal Humility

"According to Saint Augustine, to be holy is to know who God is and to know that it is not you."

"We talk a lot about how much we need each other and about how much the kids need us. But do they need us in the way we think?"

"I don't think we take the time to reverence the other's story, touch the power of it, and let the story move our spirit."

"Sometimes I feel like a bull in a china shop, and sometimes I feel like china in a bull's closet."

"Say to yourself when you get a free moment, 'I am not the Messiah.'"

B. Questioning

"Learn to use questions. Talk about issues that matter. Raise up human questions as humanly as possible. Get them to tell the real; then you'll help them see the work and will of God."

"Don't give kids your wisdom because 'they don't have it, and they need it.' What a sinful sort of approach that is! Rather, we should impose questions that enable them to enter into a relationship with the texts of their lives."

"If you think of questions and conversations as your resources—instead of statements and declarations—then you will be well on your way to fostering spiritual formation with young people."

"Sharpen your intentionality about the kinds of questions you pose . . . the kinds of conversations you want kids to engage in, so that you can be about spiritual growth. The key is having confidence in the kinds of questions you pose."

C. A Quality of Presence

"It is not what I say to kids in order to help them. I hate to say it, but it's about how I am with them and how I react to things like life and death, like the things that are important to them."

"The key for being in solidarity with kids is simply this: *reasonably honest soulfulness,* in which the events of the day and one's life are discussed and addressed by two souls, yours and theirs, in ways that matter. Find that decent, soulful side of yourself, and try to connect that to the decent, soulful, side of a kid."

"Conversation is a moral act."

"Some kids don't have money for psychologists. I know we must have sensitivity and there is a real need for professional help, but a lot of times we can make do with clear values and the sharing of what every human being needs to know."

"I tell my staff that what is most important is that kids experience and remember that when they were in our presence, they were special. When they came here they were cared for, and we were excited that they were with us."

"If we cannot hang out with [be present to] kids around their loss of innocence—from our spiritual side [with a faith perspective]— then we just add to their fears. But we must have their permission to do so" [respecting their wishes to talk or not talk about their loss of innocence, delicate situations, painful moments].

"Kids move around like they have this clear bubble surrounding them. They can see you, and you can see them. But you can't make contact with them—and they can't make contact with you—because they are inside this bubble. Too many adults try to establish a shared bubble with a kid. It's not going to happen. No kid is going to, or should, enter into a shared bubble relationship with an adult. However, with a lot of observation, you can find an occasional entry point inside that young person's bubble."

"If we seek to be imitators of Christ as the One who redeems, saves, et cetera, we will seek to solve problems. Where does that leave us when we can't, because of the immensity of it all? Perhaps the best imitation of Christ is a certain kind of presence in their midst."

"There is an ancient Sufi saying: 'Just don't do something. Stand there.'"

D. Authenticity

"People in my neighborhood know this: It is not who you are that counts the most. It's who people say you are that counts."

"When you try to help kids, don't expect people to join you. No one is going to join you. But they might help you if they think you are a person of integrity."

"It has occurred to me that hypocrisy is like air. We don't know that we are breathing it in until it is so polluted it hurts us."

"The person who is hypocritical cannot grow in their spiritual life because they make themselves prisoners of themselves."

"Authenticity is not a given. It is a verb. It is an accomplishment that takes great effort and great discipline. And authenticity does not excuse us to be rude, insensitive, or sure that we know the whole truth about a situation."

E. Comfort with Contradictions

"The key lies in the wisdom of the ration between suspicion and generosity. When you operate out of a hermeneutics of suspicion, then everything you hear, read, and encounter will be treated by skepticism and mistrust. When you operate out of a hermeneutics of generosity, then you tend to give everyone the benefit of the doubt and trust everyone. Too much of a hermeneutics of generosity will make you look like a damn fool. Too much of a hermeneutics of suspicion will make you bitter. We all need to find the wisdom of the ration between suspicion and generosity, between ordinary and extraordinary. This requires discernment of the Spirit. Suspicion helps us challenge; generosity helps us support."

"I'm not clear as to how to walk the tightrope of using my moral voice and my moral authority and at the same time shutting up and working hard at listening to kids."

"I love the kid who was shot. . . . And I loved the kid who shot him."

"You have to be able to hold the paradoxes and the contradictions, like having tired feet . . . standing in the promised land."

"Some problems should not be solved too quickly. Stay in relationship with the contradictions for a while."

F. Personal Support

"We have discovered that those who are living lives committed to others are not 'lone rangers.' They may appear to be, but we have found that they all have a communion of saints made up of humility and chutzpah."

"Faith is, in part, a matter of the company we keep. All of us need networks of belonging and a mentoring community."

"The crux of the problem is this: Instead of compartmentalizing our work by issues, we need to talk to people who look at us and ask, 'What do you stand for morally and spiritually?'"

"Don't hang out at the CNB club with those who just *complain, nag,* and *bitch.*"

"To do what we have to do, we have to lean on each other and learn from each other. But we can't do what we need to do if we don't tell each other."

"We all need a community—as small as one or two people."

"You have to have some friends, or at least one other person you can trust. You can stand in place within an environment of mistrust, but you can't dance there. The same for kids. Spiritually speaking, where, when, and with whom can they dance with God?"

G. Resourcefulness

"Fidelity to kids is not enough. Integrity is not enough. You have to be faithful AND creative."

"You can be compassionate all you want, but if you don't do something significant and specific, then forget it."

"I did what experts told me once. I referred this girl's situation to a child protection service. That night her dad beat the hell out of her. I can still see her with those bruises all over her body when she came to school the next day. I don't follow the rules exactly like that anymore."

"It takes whatever it takes."

"I'm at a disadvantage. I'm advised by the police not to do home visits because it is not safe for a woman . . . so I write a lot of notes to kids. It's amazing what that does for your relationship with kids.

"Sometimes a lily grows in a cesspool. Find and define the seed."

H. Reverence for Family

"If you are going to measure young people who are addicted or mean, measure them right. At some point, not long ago, they were somebody's baby. At some point, not long ago, they were someone's love."

"I remember always wanting to go to the Easter sunrise service as a young boy but was always told that I was too young. Then one night my dad woke me up at two o'clock in the morning and said softly, 'You're old enough.' I remember how that felt. As we walked the blocks to the church in the dark, I still remember how it felt to hold my father's hand."

"Sometimes it helps to remember that you are not just forming or informing the spirituality of the kids you work with. You are touching their children."

"The mother told me, 'Baby, you are the only one I trust because you are the only one who looks me in the eye.'"

"After he confessed to the murder and after describing each weapon and the position of each person in complete detail . . . after the confession was completely over, the detectives asked him if he had any questions, and he asked, 'Can I call my mother?'"

I. Anger

"Anger is good. I bless anger. It enables you to do what you have to do, but now we must teach people how to handle their anger."

"In researching lives committed to the common good, we had to look at anger. The spiritual fire of anger is, for many, that blue flame at the core of their soul that sustains them."

"Every time there is something that makes me sad or angry, it propels me to do something."

J. Strength of Spirit

"All some kids have is you. That's the truth, and it should make you tremble."

"You have to have an ego that is big enough to believe that the lives of kids are better because of you."

"You need to have a tender strength and a strong tenderness to those with whom you are willing to be with."

Solidarity While Teaching

Offering solidarity with adolescents includes offering a kind of solidarity with their religious questioning. Charles Shelton maintains that adolescent religious questioning is a result of their natural development. Adolescent religious questioning comes from:

1. Their increased cognitive ability to think abstractly and embrace questions such as, "Why is there evil?" and "Why do bad things happen to good people?"

2. Their increased disillusionment with adult behaviors that fail to live up to their ideals, which leads young people to question sources and wisdom of religious traditions.

3. The increased demands on their identity formation, which cause young people to question their value system.[2]

Shelton points out that attempts to give "reasonable" answers to the experiences and religious doubts of adolescents is not wise:

Pastorally speaking, it is not wise to attempt to 'solve' these types of questions for the adolescent. Although this inclination is well intended, it is nevertheless shortsighted because it deprives the adolescent of an opportunity for real growth in facing the complexities inherent in his or her own development. A more fruitful and meaningful approach is to dialog with the adolescent. . . . A helpful way to address adolescent questions about God is to not talk about whether or not God exists but, rather, about who God is.[3]

He suggests that posing this question instead of answering one regarding God's existence might lead to a discussion of love. A young person may answer with, "To me God is love." The adult might respond by asking the young person questions, such as:

- How do you love?
- How is love kept in your life?
- When is love freely given?
- To whom do you give your love?
- What is the power of love?
- How is love abused?
- How is God's love present?
- What is the power of God's love?
- When is God's love abused?

Offering solidarity in this way requires that interested adults respect the views of young people, engage adolescents at both the affective and cognitive level, encourage young people to stay open and reflective as they process their thoughts, feelings, and experiences, and lovingly challenge them to take responsibility for their questions, ideas, responses, and behaviors.[4]

Psychotherapists working with treatment-resistant youth also report success using group discussion of realistic moral dilemmas related to the use of alcohol or drugs, abstaining from sexual intercourse, confronting friends or family, cheating on tests, hosting a party when one's parents are away, and so on.[5]

On the other hand, sometimes the best way of offering solidarity when a young person asks us a question is to share our answers directly, clearly, and with some confidence. Offering solidarity to youth struggling with sexual activity, for example, challenges us to state clearly our religious values and the reasons those religious values make sense to us. Young people expect that we have thought this issue through. Adults owe it to young people to share the rationale for their views regarding chastity. At the same time, there is the challenge to remember that adolescent sexual activity can symbolize underlying adolescent needs for affection, competence, intimacy, and so on.[6]

I have found it helpful to first ask young people when discussing premarital sexual activity, "Who gets hurt?" and "How do people get hurt?" Because young people know pain and know truth, they can honestly discuss the emotional costs of disillusionment, guilt, insincerity, betrayal, secrecy, rumors, gossip, and tarnished reputations. After young people identify and often validate the pain of premarital sexual activity, adults can *then* point to the traditional sources of wisdom, such as religious teachings, parental advice, and Scripture, and say "No wonder the Church says . . ." "No wonder your parents say . . ." "No wonder the Bible says . . ."

Adolescent spiritual growth is an integral part of the process of changing one's lifestyle. Offering solidarity for spiritual growth includes staying with adolescents as they attempt to make significant change. Frederic Craigie maintains that "Literature on Christian counseling may be said to reveal two themes about the process of change. First, individuals change as a result of *solving problems*. . . . Second, individuals change as a result of growth in faithfulness and vitality of Christian discipleship."[7]

Offering solidarity with adolescents can result in a trusting relationship in which young people present adults with the challenge to *lead* their spiritual growth. Ronald Heifetz, in *Leadership Without Easy Answers,* offers several leadership activities that apply directly to the task of offering the kind of solidarity that eventually presents the opportunity to lead.

1. *Identify the adaptive challenge:* Point out to young people the specific behavior one is trying to promote or change. The key concept here is to remind them that *there is work to be done in order to grow.*

2. *Regulate distress:* Make your presence a holding environment, wherein you provide a safe place for adolescents to state their opinions without ridicule but provide enough struggle, complexity, and time limits to engage, stimulate, and challenge young people to wrestle with, and apply, what they know is needed. Like cooking on a stove, keep your hand on the heat regulator to keep the learning process percolating—without boiling over.

3. *Direct attention to the issues:* Maintain a disciplined focus on the challenge or discovery at hand and the behavior to be promoted or

changed. Keep young people paying attention to the truth or action under discussion.

4. *Give the work back to the people:* Don't take a shortcut by doing the work for the adolescents with whom you are in solidarity. Help, guide, challenge, and keep young people focused, but let them complete the activity themselves and hold them accountable for uncompleted activities or poorly practiced situations.

5. *Protect voices of those lacking authority:* Give cover to the adolescents who raise tough questions, provoke alternative thinking, challenge norms, and yet lack recognition among their peers.

6. *Pay attention to the pace:* If things seem to be moving too fast, slow them down. If the pace seems to be dragging, then speed it up and add some positive stress or complexity of insight to the situations. Pace is important to kids. The speed of processing situations with adolescents can have a negative or positive impact on productivity.

7. *Come to the balcony:* Take time out to analyze what it's like "on the dance floor" of your relationship with young people by giving yourself occasions to be a reflective practitioner. Take a confidant and a partner with you. Make time to mentally step away and be an observer of the dance between you and the young people for whom you care. Also, make your presence serve as a "balcony" by providing opportunities for young people to reflect on the dancing in their own lives.[8]

FOR REFLECTION

1. Pick three of the situations that open this chapter and identify how you would offer solidarity in each one.

2. Of the nine areas of solidarity presented in this chapter, which two do you find yourself most interested in?

3. Of all the statements made by those quoted in this chapter, which ones strike you the most? Why?

4. Which of the adult attributes listed in this chapter are yours?

5. Which of the attributes do you wish you could develop more fully?

6. On a scale of one to ten, with ten being the highest, how would you rate your level of comfort with adolescent questioning?

7. How frequently do you "come to the balcony"? In what ways do you "come to the balcony"? Who do you want to take with you as a confidant the next time you "come to the balcony"?

8. Has the reading of this book served to take you to the balcony in any way? If so, what have you observed from your position on the balcony about the way you have offered solidarity to adolescents?

PRACTICALLY SPEAKING

*   Recognize that which makes up *the dream* in the heart of the adolescents with whom you work. Then recognize the obstacles that threaten the dream. These are the matters about which you can offer solidarity. It's that simple.
*   A simple way to literally offer solidarity to a young person is to ask, "How's your life on a scale of one to ten these days?" If he or she responds with an eight or higher, simply smile and say something like, "That's great. I'm jealous!!!" If the response is seven or less, you might say, "Sounds kind of low. What's up?" The young person's response to your second question will indicate whether or not he or she accepts your offer of solidarity.
*   Do not act or talk like an adolescent's "older buddy." He or she needs and wants you to be an *adult who cares,* not a peer.

- Demonstrate *both* tenderness and strength, not just one. You need both, like two arms, to fully embrace the spirituality of teens.
- *Always* be honest. If you can't say something without embarrassing another person, then explain that "I can't talk about that" or "I'd rather not go there."
- Smile, laugh, and enjoy a sense of humor when something funny happens or is said. While children fret, adolescents worry. Seeing humor and laughter in adulthood helps teens relax, gain perspective, and imagine adulthood in a healthier way.
- While most conversations with adolescents can, and should, happen while doing two or three other things at the same time, look directly into the young person's eyes when you really want to emphasize a point. Ask the adolescent to look at you as well.

Chapter 6

Being an Intrusive Presence

There is a collision in the night
And we are it.
There is a grappling before dawn
And we are there.
There is the temptation to put our heads into the lion's mouth
And it should not be tamed.
There is a fury in the soul
And that is our chance.

attributed to Phil Cousineau, poet and author[1]

Traditionally, the privilege of facilitating spiritual growth among adolescents has been exercised only by those trained in theology, spiritual direction, and/or the sacred writings and rituals of their religion. However, the three-dimensional understanding of spirituality and the four different kinds of activities outlined in this book provide specific ways for interested adults to participate in the spiritual growth of adolescents without formal training. The strength of the model we have explored is this: *Anyone* can participate in the spiritual growth of young people. All that is required is integrity, faith, and respect for young people.

Three-Dimensional Spirituality

Understanding that adolescent spirituality comprises three dimensions—religious faith, moral living, and emotional awareness—enables caring adults to see the spiritual value of their work with adolescents. These three dimensions are distinct and interrelated. A person possessing only a strong religious dimension resembles the Pharisees of Jesus' day. A person possessing only a strong moral dimension resembles the altruistic agnostic. In the extreme, a person possessing only emotional awareness resembles those who are emotionally in control but who do not invest in helping others (moral living) or in their relationship with God (religious faith).

The three-dimensional view of spirituality enables adults (and youth) to glimpse, mark, and work with a specific area of a young person's development. This view of spirituality implies that religious faith alone does not make for an integrated spiritual life. Moral living—a constitutive and non-negotiable dimension of spirituality—is equally essential. The third dimension—emotional awareness—helps overcome obstacles to moral living and religious faith, while also showing young people that which their hearts hold to be most sacred.

This three-dimensional view of spirituality encourages the coach to see the spiritual value of helping athletes handle their anger appropriately, demonstrate good sportsmanship, recover from failure, and handle the pain of loss. Emotional awareness of this sort enhances young people's ability to live out the moral dimensions of their spirituality.

Such a view similarly encourages the high school guidance counselor to see the spiritual value of helping young people reflect on the moral quality of their relationships and decisions. Public school teachers can see the specific contribution they make to the spiritual growth of young people when they promote character development because, even though moral living is a constitutive dimension of spiritual growth, it does not require one to speak in religious terms.

Ironically, the three-dimensional view of spirituality enables theological teachers, ministers, rabbis, and other religious leaders to accept the value of their contribution to the religious growth of adolescents through worship and doctrinal studies without feeling obliged to *excel* in their ability to work with the specifics of youth culture and its impact on adolescents' moral lives.

Parents, grandparents, relatives, guardians, and mentors—all of us—can participate in the development of any or all three dimensions of a young person's spiritual growth by paying new attention to the way young people express each of these three dimensions of their spirituality. In this way, adults can improve their ability to recognize the dominant dimension of a young person's spirituality and seek to nurture the less-developed dimensions.

For example, a young person whose dominant dimension of spirituality is religious faith is likely to say something like:

"God and I are tight (close). I pray all the time, especially when I'm in trouble or need help. I pray every night, and I think about God a lot during the day. I even go to Sunday school and ask questions about God. My relationship with God is important."

In statements like these, there is little mention of the challenges of moral living and the call to contribute to the well-being of others.

A young person with a dominant moral dimension might signal this fact with comments such as:

> *"For me, faith is really about helping other people. I believe in God and that God is watching over me, but I don't go to church much or pray a lot. I really think that God wants me to be a good friend and a good listener and to pay attention to those who get excluded or made fun of. My faith calls me to be fair and honest and not to be prejudiced."*

Paying attention to the spirituality of adolescents in this way enables adults, family members, and friends to recognize teachable moments and make gentle initiatives that affirm the dominant dimension(s) of a young person's spirituality, while also intentionally investing in the less-dominant dimension(s).

Four Activities for Spiritual Growth

We have explored four specific activities: attending to stories, building skills, honoring the senses, and offering solidarity. Two points can be made.

1. These four activities correspond to the cognitive, behavioral, affective, and interpersonal domains of spiritual formation.

2. You and others can participate in the activities most compatible to your particular abilities, interests, styles, settings, and relationships with youth.

Attending to stories involves the cognitive function of processing the details of stories and exploring their spiritual themes (in light of the dimensions of religious faith, moral living, and emotional awareness). We can engage in this activity in formal settings, such as classrooms, retreat centers, and church youth groups. We also can attend to stories in more informal ways, such as while riding in a car, while carrying on a one-to-one conversation in a hallway about a movie or a song, or while eating from paper plates at a family gathering. The stories discussed can be the sacred sagas and parables of one's religious tradition, with emphasis on identifying the story's religious doctrines or moral precepts. Stories told on video, television, or film also can be used to uncover moral principles, emotional awareness, and/or religious truths. Family legends, current events, and the stories resulting from the experiences of young people also provide abundant opportunities for discussions, discoveries, and affirmations regarding spiritual growth.

Building skills is the activity that emphasizes behaviors or even practices of a religious, moral, and emotional nature. Of the four activities described in this work, building skills is the most formal and technical. Building skills requires practice and a certain degree of structure. Building skills relies more on the ability of the adult to be instructional. Unlike the other three activities, building skills requires us to plan and prepare the best method to use with adolescents and the clearest way to explain the steps involved in particular skills. This activity may be the one most appealing to those of us who possess the ability to instruct or "coach" in this fashion. Of the four activities explored, the notion of building skills for spiritual growth represents new ground and begs for further development. There is great potential to develop and teach young people even more skills than those listed in this book.

Honoring the senses—particularly when emotionality and imagination are involved—respects and depends upon the adolescent's ability to *recognize* the truth, *image* mystery, *articulate* the holy, *sense* the sacred, *appreciate* beauty, and *respond to* goodness. Those of us wishing to engage in this activity among young people can begin by listening to the ways in which young people describe their religious, moral, and emotional experiences and by paying attention to the intensity with which these experiences are described. In addition, we can engage in honoring the senses by using secular and sacred symbols, images, metaphors, and analogies in our work with young people.

It is important to remember that adolescent emotionality holds clues to the deeply held values, dreams, and passions of young people. You can help adolescents discover that which their hearts hold most sacred by enabling them to look at the root causes of their emotions.

Offering solidarity is exclusively centered around the kinds of relationships that we can establish with adolescents in order to help them handle the different tasks related to religious faith, moral living, and emotional awareness. This activity centers around the ways we become companions to and mentor adolescents without imposing ourselves on young people or robbing them of opportunities to exercise their own voice, solve their own problems, or make their own contributions. It makes important distinctions between "standing in solidarity," "being in solidarity," and "offering solidarity."

Those of us wishing to engage in offering solidarity should possess certain relational qualities, some of which may appear to be in opposition to each other, such as ego strength *and* humility. On the other hand, the activity of offering solidarity does not require one to have the same affective sensitivity as those engaged in honoring the senses, the instructional ability of those engaged in building skills, or the style of those engaged in attending to stories.

Doing Well

It should also be noted that this work intentionally avoids activities aimed at building self-esteem by offering young people nonspecific affirmation and praise. As mentioned in an earlier chapter, it is not helpful to implement approaches on the assumption that *if kids feel good (about themselves), they will do well.* Instead, we may find it far more helpful to use approaches that assume that *if kids do well, they will feel good (about themselves).*

Young people will do well in the three dimensions of their spirituality—religious faith, moral living, and emotional awareness—with the help of adults who intentionally engage, and thereby *teach,* them by attending to stories, building skills, honoring the senses, and offering solidarity.

Young people will do well when they enjoy a sense of discovery at the truths they find embedded in stories. They will do well when they enjoy a sense of competence as they see themselves growing in three different sets of skills for spiritual growth. They will do well when they enjoy a growing and varied sense of God's presence and when they find solidarity offered by adults they can trust.

When young people do well through spiritual growth of this sort, they become able to cope successfully with the challenges of contemporary life and to contribute to the common good. Doing well in this way addresses matters of the adolescent spirit.

The work and privilege of embracing the spiritual growth of adolescents can be enhanced in the third millennium by fresh and intentional efforts to implement and record the impact of attending to stories, building skills, honoring the senses, and/or offering solidarity to adolescents. Future field-based research of this kind may produce insights as to:

- specific techniques that may be helpful when engaging in each or any of these four activities;
- skills needed by adults engaged in any of these four activities;
- the optimal or minimal time needed to engage adolescents in any of these activities so that they are effective;
- a description of the kinds of settings that seem most conducive to these four activities.

In addition, young people can be interviewed in an effort to:

- gather a profile of their religious imagination within contemporary culture;
- identify their spiritual moments;
- determine specific skills that they most desire for spiritual growth;
- ascertain the kind of adult solidarity most appealing to them.

The four activities we have explored all begin with the letter *S:* stories, skills, sense, and solidarity. However, one other activity beginning with the letter *S* should be the subject of further discussion and research because it, too, seems to be a doorway to the spirituality of adolescents—service. Exploring questions such as the following can provide us with important direction:

- What is it about this activity that enriches the religious, moral, and emotional dimensions of adolescent spirituality?
- What should we keep in mind as we provide and participate in service with young people?

Meanwhile, the content within these pages may be shared with parents, teachers, youth workers, clergy, and all adults interested in adolescent spiritual growth for the purpose of generating discussion that points out the strengths and limits of both this book and/or one's own efforts and ideas.

Because the four activities presented—attending to stories, building skills, honoring the senses, and offering solidarity—lend themselves to different skills, functions, and settings, each one of us may explore which activity best suits our particular abilities and interests. Therein lies the greatest value of the approach, which is worth repeating: All adults can participate, provided that they are people of integrity and faith who have respect for young people.

In the end, the model that we have explored for embracing the spirituality of adolescents offers caring adults several specific ways to be an intrusive presence in the lives of young people. An intrusive presence is not obtrusive or oppressive. It is a presence that is gently and consistently in the face of young people, taking them deeper and more quickly into conversations that matter, helping them recognize the movement and love of God in their lives while also holding them close, keeping them accountable.

For any caring adult, to be an intrusive presence is to be a partner with God in a relationship that embraces the spirituality of young people. It is simple, but not easy. Sometimes we dance, and sometimes we wrestle.[2]

We began with a story that may have helped us think about the approaches we each have to "fishing the river." I would like to close with another story about fishing—one that I hope will enable you to think more about being an intrusive presence long after reading the printed words.

> *I love to fish. Every year I go to my favorite fishing spot to spend time there. It is always an occasion of prayer for me. Because I am involved in the spiritual growth of adolescents, I often recall the Lord's invitation to be fishers of men, I mean, folks.*
>
> *One day while I was fishing by this very large lake, the Lord looked down upon me from heaven and said to Saint Peter, "Hey, Rocky, Mike has found a decent fishing spot. Want to go fishing?" Everybody knows that Saint Peter's nickname in heaven is Rocky. It had to do with being a rock upon which someone was going to build a house, a church, a gymnasium, or some such edifice. Anyway, Peter was excited. He said, "Oh, Lord, I'd love to go! I used to be a heck of an angler. I mean to tell you, I could **really fish!** It's been around two thousand years*

since I've been fishing, and even though that's not more than a couple of days for us up here, I'd love to go!"

Then the two of them dropped in on me, but I wasn't happy about it. No angler likes to share a special place with uninvited guests. However, given who these two guys were, I was gracious. I shook their hands and said, "My, Lord, it's good to see you" and "Hello, Saint Peter, nice to meet you." They were both very friendly.

Peter had brought just one lure with him. He held it out and bragged, "This is my favorite lure. Always catches fish. Can't miss!" It had Made in Galilee *written underneath it.*

Now the Lord was a sight. He looked like he had read every magazine about fishing and believed every word. He was wearing a hat on which were stuck all kinds of lures, plus a few buttons from past presidential campaigns pinned on for good luck. He had on a vest that must have had twelve pockets. There were zippers everywhere! And around his neck dangled a nail clippers hung on shoestring.

Here's what happened. The two of them rowed out on the lake in a simple little boat. Peter sat in the middle of the boat and fished with his Made in Galilee *special. I fished from the bank, as always. But the Lord was different. He fished all over the boat. Sometimes he would fish in the front of the boat, sometimes in the back, sometimes from one side of the boat, sometimes from the other side. He would sometimes use a lure that he could throw really far, and sometimes he would use a tiny, light lure that he dropped gently and quietly onto the water. It seemed that he changed his lure every fifteen minutes. That's why he had the clippers hung around his neck—to clip the line each time he tied on a new lure. Sometimes, he would reel in his lure hard and fast across the top of the water's surface, making it splash along the way. Sometimes, he would use a very heavy lure and just drop it straight down deep and bob the lure off the bottom of the lake.*

Peter sat in the same spot in the boat the entire time, fishing Made in Galilee. *I kept fishing from the bank.*

Around lunchtime the Lord stopped fishing. He opened up a Kosher turkey sandwich and a cold bottle of something to drink. After his lunch he laid down in the boat, pulled his hat over his eyes, and took a nap. Peter and I kept fishing. We didn't even stop for lunch but just ate with one hand and fished with the other.

After his nap the Lord did more of the same: front of the boat, back of the boat, long casts, short casts, lures that ran on top of the water, lures that ran down deep on the bottom, lures requiring slow retrieves, and lures requiring fast, splashy ones; left side, right side, he changed lures often. Around three o'clock the Lord and Peter started packing up the fishing gear.

When they got to the shore, I said, "Lord, I've been fishing this lake for a long time and never have I seen anyone fish your way. What's the deal?" He had caught fifteen fish, and Peter had caught five. I hadn't caught any, but I had this HUGE fish on my line, which broke. It must have been huge. . . .

The Lord said, "I always let the weather and water conditions dictate how I fish. When we first went out this morning, the water was still cold, so I used a lure that would swim on the top of the surface because I knew the fish would be in the water closest to the warm sun. As the day went on, and the water got warmer, I used a lure that would run down deep, where the fish were enjoying cooler water. When the tide ran hard to the right, I fished on the left side of the boat with a lure that I could reel in hard so that it could swim against the tide instead of getting swept away. When the tide ran left, I switched to the right side of the boat.

"When I came upon muddy water, I fished with a bright lure that fish could see. When I came upon clear water, I fished with a lure that would blend in so as not to scare them away. When the sky got cloudy, I fished with one kind of lure. When it was bright and sunny, I tried a different kind. When I came upon still pools of water, I used a gentle lure that would not make a disturbance and frighten the fish. When the water was choppy, I used a more rugged lure. See, I always let the weather and water conditions dictate how I fish.

"Now, Peter did okay I guess, but Mike, your choosing to fish from the bank. . . ." Looking down, the Lord sort of shook his head without finishing his sentence. Then he looked at me and said, *"Remember what you saw today, for so it is with being—and not being—an intrusive presence in the lives of kids."*

Then Peter started to blurt out, "And those who have ears to hear . . . ," but before he could finish, they both disappeared.

I wonder what the Lord meant? Do you know?

Notes

Chapter 1

1. Wade C. Roof, *A Generation of Seekers: The Spiritual Journeys of the Baby Boom Generation* (San Francisco: HarperSanFrancisco, 1993).
2. Robert Kegan, "There the Dance Is: Religious Dimensions of Developmental Theory," in *Toward Moral and Religious Maturity,* eds. James Fowler and Antoine Vergote (Morristown, NJ: Silver Burdett, 1980).
3. Craig Dykstra and Sharon Parks, eds., *Faith Development and Fowler* (Birmingham, AL: Religious Education Press, Inc., 1986); Charles M. Shelton, *Morality of the Heart: A Psychology for the Christian Moral Life* (New York: Crossroad Publishing Co., 1997).
4. Robert Kegan, *In Over Our Heads: The Mental Demands of Modern Life* (Cambridge, MA: Harvard University Press, 1995).
5. David Elkind, *All Grown Up and No Place to Go: Teenagers in Crisis* (Reading, MA: Addison-Wesley Longman, Inc., 1998).
6. Fred M. Hechinger, *Fateful Choices: Healthy Youth for the Twenty-First Century* (New York: Hill & Wang, 1993); Daniel Goleman, *Emotional Intelligence: Why It Can Matter More than IQ* (New York: Bantam Books, 1997); Martin E. Seligman, *The Optimistic Child: A Proven Program to Safeguard Children Against Depression and Build Lifelong Resilience* (New York: HarperTrade, 1997).
7. Hechinger, *Fateful Choices: Healthy Youth for the Twenty-First Century,* 217.
8. *The Five Promises.* America's Promise, http://www.americaspromise.org/FivePromises/FivePromises.cfm.
9. Robert Kegan, *The Evolving Self: Problem and Process in Human Development* (Cambridge, MA: Harvard University Press, 1983).
10. Charles M. Shelton, *Adolescent Spirituality: Pastoral Ministry for High School and College Youth* (New York: Crossroad Publishing Co., 1989), 125.
11. Henri Nouwen, *Out of Solitude: Three Meditations on the Christian Life* (Notre Dame, IN: Ave Maria Press, 1974), 21–22.
12. Robert Coles, *The Spiritual Life of Children* (New York: Houghton Mifflin Co., 1990).

13. James W. Fowler, *Stages of Faith: The Psychology of Human Development* (San Francisco: HarperSanFrancisco, 1995).

14. Shelton, *Adolescent Spirituality: Pastoral Ministry for High School and College Youth.*

15. Mike Carotta, *Catholic and Capable: Skills for Spiritual Growth* (Allen, TX: Resources for Christian Living, 1998).

16. Sara P. Little, *To Set One's Heart: Belief and Teaching in the Church* (Louisville, KY: Westminster John Knox Press, 1986).

17. Wilfred C. Smith, *The Meaning and End of Religion* (Minneapolis: Augsburg Fortress Publishers, 1990).

18. Thomas H. Groome, *Christian Religious Education: Sharing Our Story and Vision* (San Francisco: Jossey-Bass, Inc. Publishers, 1999).

19. Peter L. Benson, Dorothy L. Williams, and Arthur L. Johnson, *The Quicksilver Years: The Hopes and Fears of Early Adolescence* (San Francisco: HarperSanFrancisco, 1987), 118.

20. Coles, *The Spiritual Life of Children.*

21. Roof, *A Generation of Seekers: The Spiritual Journeys of the Baby Boom Generation,* 76–77.

22. William Damon, *The Moral Child: Nurturing Children's Natural Moral Growth* (New York: The Free Press, 1990); Norma Haan, Elaine Aerts, and Bruce A. Cooper, *On Moral Grounds: The Search for Practical Morality* (New York: New York University Press, 1988); Thomas Lickona, *Educating for Character: How Our Schools Can Teach Respect and Responsibility* (New York: Bantam Books, 1992); Alasdair C. MacIntyre, *After Virtue: A Study in Moral Theory* (Notre Dame, IN: University of Notre Dame Press, 1984); Charles M. Shelton, *Morality of the Heart: A Psychology for the Christian Moral Life* (New York: Crossroads Publishing Co., 1997).

23. Peter Salovey and John Mayer, "Emotional Intelligence," *Imagination, Cognition, and Personality* 9 (1990): 185–211.

24. Goleman, *Emotional Intelligence: Why It Can Matter More than IQ.*

25. Seligman, *The Optimistic Child: A Proven Program to Safeguard Children Against Depression and Build Lifelong Resilience.*

26. Robert Coles, "Verbal Consultation and Feedback on the Design of *Catholic and Capable*" (1995).

27. Aristotle, J. E. Welldon, trans., *The Nicomachean Ethics* (Amherst, NY: Prometheus Books, U.S., 1987), 54.

28. Mary Brabeck, ed., *Who Cares: Theory, Research, and Educational Implications of the Ethic of Care* (Westport, CT: Praeger Publishers, 1989).

29. Damon, *The Moral Child*, 116.

30. Ibid., 117–118.

Chapter 2

1. Barry Lopez, *Crow and Weasel* (New York: Farrar, Straus, Giroux, LLC, 1990), 48.

2. K. Welsch, "Popular Periodicals and Rhetoric and Composition Textbooks in the Nineteenth Century: A Cultural Conversation on Composing Oneself" (paper presented at the annual meeting of the Conference of College Composition and Communication, Washington, D.C., March 23–25, 1995).

3. G. Brennan, "Telling Stories in School: The Ancient Art of Storytelling," *Times Educational Supplement* 2, (1995): 55–56; Robert Coles, *The Call of Stories: Stories and the Moral Imagination* (New York: Houghton Mifflin Co., 1990); M. Culp, "Literature's Influence on Young Adult Attitudes, Values, and Behavior, 1975 and 1984," *English Journal* 74 (1985): 31–36; Stanley Hauerwas, "The Difference of Virtue and the Difference It Makes: Courage Exemplified," *Modern Theology* 9 (1993): 249–265.

4. K. Egan, "Young Children's Imagination and Learning: Engaging Children's Emotional Response," *Young Children* 49 (1994): 27–32; Janet Hall, *Confident Kids: Helping Your Child Cope with Fear* (Port Melbourne, VIC AUS: Lothian Publishing Co., 1995); R. Ma, "Storytelling as a Teaching-Learning Strategy: A Nonnative Instructor's Perspective" (paper presented at the annual Speech Communication Association, New Orleans, November 19–22, 1994); K. Prial, *Literary Reflections on Personal and Social Change: A Language Arts Unit for Grades 4–6* (Williamsburg, VA: College of William and Mary, 1994); J. Snowman, "Research Alive: All Our Children Learning," *Mid-Westerner Educational Researcher* 7 (1994): 30–34; Sandra Wilde and David J. Whitin, *It's the Story That Counts: More Children's Books for Mathematical Learning, K–6* (Westport, CT: Heinemann, 1995).

5. J. Frick, *Multicultural Studies: Final Report, Curriculum and Stories* (Warminster, PA: Partners for English As a Second Language, Inc.,

1994); D. Hodges, "Creation Stories: Windows to Cultural Values," *Interdisciplinary Humanities* 12 (1995): 3–9; D. Mahala and J. Swilky, "Rhetoricizing the Teacher's Position: Or What to Make of the Ghost of 'Process,' in Multicultural Pedagogies" (paper presented at the annual meeting of the Conference of College Composition and Communication, Washington, D.C., March 23–25, 1995).

6. A. Bowman, "Teaching Ethics: Telling Stories," *Nurse Education Today* 15 (1995): 33–38.

7. F. Connelly and D. Clandinin, "Telling Teaching Stories," *Teacher Education Quarterly* 21 (1994): 145–58.

8. F. English and B. Steffy, "Using Film to Attain a Cultural and Contextual Understanding of Moral Leadership" (paper presented at the annual meeting of the American Educational Research Association, April 18–22, 1995).

9. Leland Ryken, "'With Many Such Parables': The Imagination as a Means of Grace," *Bibliotheca Sacra* 147 (1990): 387–398.

10. William J. Bennett, *The Book of Virtues: A Treasury of the World's Great Moral Stories* (New York: Simon and Schuster Trade, 1993).

11. Elizabeth B. Saenger, *Exploring Ethics Through Children's Literature* (Atlanta: Council For Spiritual and Ethical Education [CSEE], 1993).

12. William Kilpatrick, *Books That Build Character: A Guide to Teaching Your Child Moral Values Through Stories* (New York: Simon and Schuster Trade Paperbacks, 1994).

13. Coles, *The Call of Stories: Stories and the Moral Imagination.*

14. S. Wisely and E. Lynn, "Spirited Connections: Learning to Tap the Spiritual Resources in Our Lives and Work," in *Spirit at Work: Discovering the Spirituality in Leadership,* ed. Jay A. Congar (San Francisco: Jossey-Bass, Inc. Publishers, 1994).

15. J. Lawrence, "Poetry and Ethics: Their Unification in the Sublime," *Southern Humanities Review* 24 (1990): 1–15; R. Seamon, "The Story of the Moral: The Function of Thematizing in Literary Criticism," *The Journal of Aesthetics and Art Criticism* 47 (1989): 229–238; S. Thomas, "Bible Belt: The Old Testament as a Cross-Curricular Resource," *Times Educational Supplement,* March 19, 1993; L. Tirrell, "Storytelling and Moral Agency," *The Journal of Aesthetics and Art Criticism* 48 (1990): 115–128; C. Vanderplas-Holper, "Children's Books and Films as Media for Moral Education: Some

Cognitive-Developmentally Orientated Considerations," *School Psychology International* 11 (1990): 31–38.

16. J. Day, "Narrative, Psychology, and Moral Education," *The American Psychologist* 46 (1991): 167–69; R. Gerrig, "Moral and Aesthetic Responses to Narratives," *The American Psychologist* 46 (1991): 165–67; D. Johnson and S. Goldman, "Children's Recognition and Use of Rules of Moral Conduct in Stories," *American Journal of Psychology* 100 (1987): 205–225; MacIntyre, *After Virtue*; Paul C. Vitz, "The Use of Stories in Moral Development: New Psychological Reasons for an Old Education Method," *American Psychologist* 45 (1990): 709–720.

17. A. Hynes and L. Wedl, "Bibliotheraphy: An Interactive Process in Counseling Older Persons," *Journal of Mental Health Counseling* 12 (1990): 288–302.

18. W. Bole, "Books Better than Bars When It Comes to Reforming Lawbreakers," *National Catholic Reporter,* August 9, 1996.

19. Ibid.

20. Edward Hayes, "Banjo Dancin,'" in *Twelve and One-Half Keys to the Gates of Paradise* (Leavenworth, KS: Forest of Peace Publishing); later adapted with permission and published in *The Discovering Program* by Mike Carotta (Winona, MN: St. Mary's Press, 1999).

21. G. Kilcourse, "Thomas Merton on Literature's 'Naked Spiritual Reserves,' "*Thought: A Review of Culture and Idea* 66 (1991): 127–138.

22. Michael Barnes, "Religion and Science: Focusing the Light of Imagination," *Word and World* 5 (1985): 240–247.

23. Catherine Madsen, "Imagination, the Poets' God," *Cross Currents* 43 (1993): 47–59.

24. Vigen Guroian, *Tending to the Heart of Virtue: How Classic Stories Awaken a Child's Moral Imagination* (New York: Oxford Press, 1998), 27.

25. J. Henry, *Holistic Teaching Strategies for Hispanic Students* (Lebanon, PA: Lebanon County Housing Authority, 1991); Rae Wyshynski and Diane Paulsen, "Maybe I Will Do Something: Lessons from Coyote," *Language Arts* 72 (1995): 258–266.

26. Edward P. Wimberly, "Pastoral Counseling with African American Men," *The Urban League Review* 16 (1993): 77–86.

27. Ellen B. Kimmel and Barbara W. Kazanis, "Explorations of the Unrecognized Spirituality of Women's Communion," *Women & Therapy* 16 (1995): 215–228; Jenefer Robinson and Stephanie Ross, "Woman, Morality, and Fiction," *Hypatia* 5 (1990): 76–90.

28. Carol Gilligan, *In a Different Voice: Psychological Theory and Women's Development* (Cambridge, MA: Harvard University Press, 1993).

29. Ibid.

30. M. E. Waithe, "Twenty-Three Hundred Years of Women Philosophers: Toward a Gender Undifferentiated Moral Theory," in *Who Cares? Theory, Research, and Educational Implications of the Ethic of Care,* ed. Mary Brabeck (Westport, CT: Praeger Publishers, 1989), 3–18.

31. Brabeck, *Who Cares?*

32. Bill Puka, "The Liberation of Caring: A Different Voice for Gilligan's 'Different Voice,'" in *Who Cares? Theory, Research, and Educational Implications of the Ethic of Care,* ed. Mary Brabeck (Westport, CT: Praeger Publishers, 1989), 9–44.

33. Carlene Seigfried, "Pragmatism, Feminism, and Sensitivity to Context," in *Who Cares? Theory, Research, and Educational Implications of the Ethic of Care,* ed. Mary Brabeck (Westport, CT: Praeger Publishers, 1989), 63–83.

34. John Dewey, "Context and Thought," in *On Experience, Nature, and Freedom,* ed. R. Bernstein (Indianapolis: Liberal Arts Press, 1960), 88–110.

35. Mary Pipher, *Reviving Ophelia: Saving the Selves of Adolescent Girls* (New York: Ballantine Publishing Group, 1999).

36. Nell Noddings, *Caring: A Feminine Approach to Ethics and Moral Education* (Berkeley, CA: University of California Press, 1984).

37. J. G. Allen and D. M. Haccoun, "Sex Differences in Emotionality: A Multidimensional Approach," *Human Relations* 29 (1976): 711–720; D. W. Birnbaum and B. E. Chelmelski, "Preschoolers' Inferences about Gender and Emotions: The Mediation of Emotionality Stereotypes," *Sex Roles* 10 (1984): 505–511; Leslie Brody, "Gender Differences in Emotional Development: A Review of Theories and Research," *Journal of Personality* 53 (1985): 102–149.

38. Theodore D. Kemper, *A Social Interactional Theory of Emotions* (New York: John Wiley and Sons, Inc., 1978); Michael Lewis and Linda Michalson, eds. *Children's Emotions and Moods:*

Developmental Theory and Measurement (Cambridge, MA: Plenum Trade, 1983).

39. N. Eisenberg, R. Fabes, and C. Shea, "Gender Differences in Empathy and Prosocial Moral Reasoning: Empirical Investigations," in *Who Cares? Theory, Research, and Educational Implications of the Ethic of Care,* ed. Mary Brabeck (Westport, CT: Praeger Publishers, 1989), 127–143.

40. D. Baumrind, "Sex Differences in Moral Reasoning: Response to Walker's (1984) Conclusion That There Are None," *Child Development* 57 (1986): 511–521; M. Brabeck, "Moral Judgement: Theory and Research on Differences Between Males and Females," *Developmental Review* 3 (1983): 274–291; James R. Rest, *Development in Judging Moral Issues* (Minneapolis: University of Minnesota Press, 1979); L. J. Walker, "Sex Differences in the Development of Moral Reasoning: A Rejoinder to Baumrind," *Child Development* 55 (1989): 677–91.

41. N. Eisenberg, R. Fabes, and C. Shea, "Gender Differences in Empathy and Prosocial Moral Reasoning: Empirical Investigations," in *Who Cares? Theory, Research, and Educational Implications of the Ethic of Care,* ed. Mary Brabeck (Westport, CT: Praeger Publishers, 1989), 127–143.

42. M. Bebeau and M. Brabeck, "Ethical Sensitivity and Moral Reasoning Among Men and Women in the Professions," in *Who Cares? Theory, Research, and Educational Implications of the Ethic of Care,* ed. Mary Brabeck (Westport, CT: Praeger Publishers, 1989), 144–163.

43. Baumrind, "Sex Differences in Moral Reasoning: Response to Walker's (1984) Conclusion That There Are None," 511–521.

44. S. Thoma, "Estimating Gender Differences in Comprehension and Preference of Moral Issues," *Developmental Review* 6 (1986): 165–180.

45. Bebeau and Brabeck, "Ethical Sensitivity and Moral Reasoning Among Men and Women in the Professions," in *Who Cares? Theory, Research, and Educational Implications of the Ethic of Care,* ed. Mary Brabeck, 144–163.

46. T. Eugene, "Sometimes I Feel Like a Motherless Child," in *Who Cares? Theory, Research, and Educational Implications of the Ethic of Care,* ed. Mary Brabeck (Westport, CT: Praeger Publishers, 1989), 45–62.

47. B. Lykes, "The Caring Self: Social Experiences of Power and Powerlessness," in *Who Cares? Theory, Research, and Educational Implications of the Ethic of Care*, ed. Mary Brabeck (Westport, CT: Praeger Publishers, 1989), 178.

48. D. Gregory, "Teaching Moral Value in the Public Schools," *Catholic Lawyer* 31 (1987): 173–182.

49. Ibid.

50. P. Legg, "Contemporary Films and Religious Exploration: An Opportunity for Religious Education (Part 1: Foundational Questions)," *Religious Education* 91 (1996): 397–406.

51. J. Laney, "Economic Concept Acquisition: Experiential Versus Experience-Based Learning and Instruction" (paper presented at the annual meeting of the National Council for the Social Studies, Nashville, TN, November 19, 1993).

52. John Shea, *Stories of God: An Unauthorized Biography* (Allen, TX: Resources for Christian Living, 1996).

Chapter 3

1. T. Everson, "Faith Skills for the Journey," *Living Light* 33 (1996): 50–58.

2. Dorothy C. Bass, ed., *Practicing Our Faith: A Way of Life for a Searching People* (San Francisco: Jossey-Bass, Inc. Publishers, 1998).

3. Carotta, *Catholic and Capable: Skills for Spiritual Growth.*

4. D. Lazear, *Seven Ways of Knowing: Teaching for Multiple Intelligences* (Arlington Heights, IL: SkyLight Training and Publishing, Inc., 1991).

5. Shelton, *Adolescent Spirituality: Pastoral Ministry for High School and College Youth,* 157.

6. Carotta, *Catholic and Capable: Skills for Spiritual Growth.*

7. William Damon, *Greater Expectations: Overcoming the Culture of Indulgence in America's Homes and Schools* (New York: The Free Press, 1996), 70–72.

8. Elisabeth Hurd, Carolyn Moore, and Randy Rogers, "Quiet Success: Parenting Strengths Among African Americans," *Families in Society: The Journal of Contemporary Human Services* 76 (1995): 434–443.

9. Damon, *Greater Expectations: Overcoming the Culture of Indulgence in America's Homes and Schools.*

10. Charles J. Sykes, *Dumbing Down Our Kids: Why American Children Feel Good about Themselves but Can't Read, Write, or Add* (New York: St. Martin's Press, LLC, 1995).

11. "Teens and Self-Image: 11th Annual Special Teen Report," *USA Weekend,* May 1–3, 1998.

Chapter 4

1. Jean-Jacques Rousseau, *Emile,* B. Foxley, trans. (London: J.M. Dent, 1974), 286.

2. Jacques Maritain, *Education at the Crossroads* (New Haven, CT: Yale University Press, 1943), 23.

3. John H. Westerhoff III, *Will Our Children Have Faith?* (Harrisburg, PA: Morehouse Publishing, 2000).

4. Fowler, *Stages of Faith: The Psychology of Human Development.*

5. Shelton, *Morality of the Heart: A Psychology for the Christian Moral Life,* 26.

6. S. Modgil and A. Modgil, eds., *Lawrence Kohlberg: Consensus and Controversy* (Philadelphia: The Falmer Press, 1985).

7. Jerome Kagan, *The Nature of the Child* (New York: Basic Books, 1994), 14.

8. Carolyn Saarni and Paul Harris, eds., *Children's Understanding of Emotion* (New York: Cambridge University Press, 1991).

9. Salovey and Mayer, "Emotional Intelligence," 185–211.

10. Goleman, *Emotional Intelligence: Why It Can Matter More than IQ.*

11. Ibid.

12. Seligman et al., *The Optimistic Child: A Proven Program to Safeguard Children Against Depression and Build Lifelong Resilience.*

13. J. Russell, "Culture, Scripts, and Children's Understanding of Emotions," in *Children's Understanding of Emotion* eds. Carolyn Saarni and Paul Harris (New York: Cambridge University Press, 1991), 300.

14. Haan, Aerts, and Cooper, *On Moral Grounds: The Search for Practical Morality,* 147.

15. Shelton, *Morality of the Heart: A Psychology for the Christian Moral Life,* 124.

16. M. Katherine Tillman, "Cardinal Newman on Imagination as the Medium of Intellectual Education," *Religious Education* 83 (1988): 601–610.

17. Maria Harris, "Completion and Faith Development," in *Faith Development and Fowler* eds. Craig Dykstra and Sharon Parks (Birmingham, AL: Religious Education Press, Inc., 1986), 115–133.

18. Sharon Parks, "Imagination and Spirit in Faith Development," in *Faith Development and Fowler* eds. Craig Dykstra and Sharon Parks (Birmingham, AL: Religious Education Press, Inc., 1986), 137–156.

19. William Chittick, "Death and the World of Imagination: Ibn al-'Arabi's Eschatology," *The Muslim World* 78 (1988): 51–82.

20. —-, "The Five Divine Presences: From al-Qunawi to al-Qaysari," *Muslim World* 72 (1982): 107–128.

21. Ryken, "'With Many Such Parables': The Imagination as a Means of Grace," 387–398.

22. George E. Tinker, "Spirituality, Native American Personhood, Sovereignty and Solidarity," *The Ecumenical Review* 44 (1992): 312–324.

23. Shelton, *Adolescent Spirituality: Pastoral Ministry for High School and College Youth.*

24. Maria Harris, *Teaching and Religious Imagination* (New York: HarperCollins Publishers, 1987).

25. Ibid.

26. Ibid.

27. Ibid.

28. D. Gouwens, "Kierkegaard on the Ethical Imagination," *Journal of Religious Ethics* 10 (1982): 204–220.

29. Harris, *Teaching and Religious Imagination,* 19–22.

30. Sharon Parks, "Social Vision and Moral Courage: Mentoring a New Generation," *Cross Currents* 40 (1990): 350–367.

31. Benedict Guevin, "The Moral Imagination and the Shaping Power of the Parables," *Journal of Religious Ethics* 17 (1989): 63–79.

32. Ibid.

33. David Loomis, "Imagination and Faith Development," *Religious Education* 83 (1988): 251–263.

34. Ibid.

35. Ibid.

36. Brenda Lealman, "Young People, Spirituality, and the Future," *Religious Education* 86 (1991): 265–74.

37. Ryken, "'With Many Such Parables': The Imagination as a Means of Grace," 387–398.

38. Max L. Stackhouse, "Ethical Vision and Musical Imagination," *Theological Education* 31 (1994): 149–163.

39. Ibid.

40. Brett Webb-Mitchell, "The Religious Imagination of Children with Disabilities," *Religious Education* 88 (1993): 305–14.

41. Ibid.

42. Paulo Freire, "The Catholic University: Reflections on Its Tasks," *Union Seminary Quarterly Review* 47 (1993): 197–201.

43. W. Lynch, "Imagining Past, Present, and Future in One Piece," *Studies in Formative Spirituality* 6 (1985): 65–72.

44. E. Hirschman and P. LaBarbera, "Dimensions of Possession Importance," *Psychology and Marketing* 7 (1990): 215–233.

45. Elkind, *All Grown Up and No Place to Go: Teenagers in Crisis.*

46. J. King, "The Moment as a Theological Category," *Studies in Formative Spirituality* 9 (1988): 79–95.

Chapter 5

1. Teaching For Spiritual Growth: A Summer Institute with Dr. Robert Coles, "nuggets" from the five annual reports included quotes from conversations with the following teachers, youth workers, and administrators:

   Year 1: Adela Acosta, Carol Brennan, Andrew J. (A. J.) Brown, Jr., Kathleen Cirillo, Christopher Evans, Joe Exline, Paul Ybarra Flores, Jeanna Forhan, Darren Foster, Lorraine Geasor, Vincent Kostos, Jim MacGillivray, Robert J. McCarthy, Mary Ann Penner, Mary Jean Raymond, Eleanor Reagan, Sharon Sani, Sean B. Scanlon, Carol Slowik, Jeffrey Smith, Marianne Supan, Stacy R. Williams.

   Year 2: Andrea Alexander, Grace M. Alexander, Michael Anderer, Gaylon Chapelle, Jeffrey Cordner, Michael B. Fabian, Kathi Frankino, Timothea Gatto, Joyce Gillie, Martha Mayne, James

Mendello, Joan Menotti, Katherine A. Murphy, Joseph Neeb, Patricia L. Neff, Gloria Nelson-Turnbow, S. Kevin Regan, Thomas Ruhland, Marcelline F. Shivers, Joan Sirois, Diana M. Solis, Martin Zemanek.

Year 3: Bob Bartlett, Joyce Smith Carter, Kathleen Dubea, Sheila Gray, Quinnette R. Igherighe, Mark Johnson, Jeanne B. Kamat, Ronald Landfair, Linda Love, Katherine McGrath, Esmeralda Perez-Gonzalez, Barb Rankin, Cathryn Rivera, Kathleen M. Ryan, Horacio Salinas, Jr., Nancy Skorko, Bob Smith, Mark Syman, Dwayne Varas, Johna Vittitow, Elliot Walker, Kathleen Yeadon.

Year 4: Group 1-Camille L. Brown, Stanley Brown, Michael Cullen, Susan Diverio, Helen Gosselin, Fred Herron, Peter Hickey, Donna Keyser, Cecilia Krause, Salvadore Lopez, Linda Lucarell-Miller, Patricia Murphy, Lorraine Pasini, Renee Pastor, Barbara Robinson, Evelin Roman, Yolanda Torres, Louis Toussant, Kevin Smith, Deanne Woods. Group 2-Diane M. Amadio, Janet Baird, Antoinette Bianco, Sharett Ann Brown, Catherine Cronin Carotta, Connie Coltrane, Richard Cunningham, Colleen Dallara, Jill Finn, Terry Furlong, Lyda Garvin, Roland Gibson, Brian Grunwald, Ilialis Hernandez, Kathleen L. Hill, Josephine King, Peggy McLaughlin, Altagracia Montas, Patricia Morris, Brenda Richardson, Gwen Richardson, Felicia Rodriquez, Fred Trainer.

Year 5: Dorene Akujobi, Benedict Baer, Donna Banfield, Carol Brown, Marjorie Butler, Javier Castillo, Charles Chesnavage, Kara Courtois, Seton Cunneen, Mary Delac, Arthur Farrington, Barbara Gargiulo, Jessica Gibson, Barbara Gorham, Joan Hartigan, Therese Jackson, Mary Keenley, William Kindall, Elizabeth Levett, Beatrice Madaj, Terese Meeks, Frank Montejano, Jamey Moses, Herbert Muralles, Mary Ann Murphy, Marcella Nolan, Barbara O'Brien-Miller, Michael Regan, Elizabeth Riehle, Leslie Roark, Rosemary Rule, Phil Trevizo.

2. Shelton, *Adolescent Spirituality: Pastoral Ministry for High School and College Youth,* 164–165.
3. Ibid.
4. Ibid.
5. John Sommers-Flanagan and Rita Sommers-Flanagan, "Psychotherapeutic Techniques with Treatment-Resistant Adolescents," *Psychotherapy* 32 (1995): 131–140.

6. Shelton, *Adolescent Spirituality: Pastoral Ministry for High School and College Youth.*
7. Frederic Craigie, "Problem-Solving, Discipleship, and the Process of Change in Christian Counseling," *Journal of Psychology and Christianity* 13 (1994): 205–216.
8. Ronald A. Heifetz, *Leadership Without Easy Answers* (Cambridge, MA: Belknap Press of Harvard University Press, 1994).

Chapter 6

1. This poem was verbally shared by a presenter at the Teaching For Spiritual Growth Summer Institute and attributed to Phil Cousineau. However, neither I nor the presenter were able to locate this poem. I reviewed all the books written or edited by Cousineau, including *Prayers at 3 A.M.: Poems, Songs, Chants, and Prayers for the Middle of the Night* (San Francisco: HarperSanFrancisco, 1995).
2. Tom Ruhland, an educator from St. Paul, Minnesota, described his faithful presence with adolescents in this way during a discussion we had at the Teaching for Spiritual Growth Institute several summers ago. I never forgot it. Years later, I asked his permission to use this phrase as the title of this work.